The Japa.

The Japan Lights

Lighthouse Carving On
Richard Henry Brunton's Gravestone,
West Norwood Cemetery

Praise for *The Japan Lights*

Iain Maloney sheds new light on the topic, with a mix of historical fact and personal touches…an entertaining, enjoyable and informative read.

Chris Glenn, radio DJ, TV presenter and author

Maloney brings a fresh twenty-first century sensibility to fellow Scotsman, engineer Richard Henry Brunton, who literally illuminated Japan's waterways in the late 1800s. Spiked with wit and sharp observations (and occasionally splashed with whisky), The Japan Lights is both entertaining and informative, like going on a series of road trips with an inquisitive friend. I will never look at a lighthouse in Japan in the same way again.

Suzanne Kamata, author of *Squeaky Wheels: Travels with My Daughter by Train, Plane, Metro, Tuk-tuk and Wheelchair*

In a kind of time-travel memoir, Iain Maloney shines a light on Brunton, illuminating both his good deeds, and his shortcomings with equal care and tenderness. Maloney's humour and compassion are the real star of the show.

Nick Bradley, author of *The Cat and The City*

Maloney takes us on a rollicking roadtrip around Japan—sometimes with his friends, sometimes alone, ofttimes with his wife—as he visits lighthouses built by the disputatious Scottish engineer Henry Brunton. Along the ride, the reader learns about the Meiji Restoration that brought foreign experts into Japan to help the nation modernize after its period of seclusion, and the cultural mishaps that accompanied this system. We learn the history behind each of Brunton's lighthouses as well as the local history of the areas surrounding them.

Amy Chavez, author of *The Widow, The Priest and the Octopus Hunter*

A kaleidoscope of a book. What begins as a road movie, Maloney travelling to remote corners of Japan, seeking out lighthouses designed by Scot Richard Brunton (appointed by the Lighthouse Stevensons), becomes a journey through his adopted homeland's geography, history, politics, culture and art. In doing so he does much the same for his native Scotland (and various other places en route!) You will never need another Japanese guide book – Maloney brings to life places few manuals will even mention. It's also a frank and witty personal memoir. 'Tour de force' is a term used too readily, but Maloney deserves it. Containing so much the book shouldn't really hang together – but it so does. By turns deeply knowledgeable and inquisitive, The Japan Lights is warm, welcoming, endlessly engrossing and entertaining.

Chris Dolan, author of *Everything Passes, Everything Remains*

Praise for *The Only Gaijin in the Village*

A charmer...the crisp, evocative prose is liberally splashed with Maloney's dry blend of humour...This book is a wealth of information and the reader learns a huge amount about rural Japan. It is charming, as is its narrator, and always amusing.

Dundee Courier 'Book of the Week'

A warm, funny, joyful experience. **Country Life**

In a world fascinated by the bright lights of Tokyo The Only Gaijin in the Village offers a new and welcome perspective of life in Japan.

Geographical Magazine

A perfect read for the novice of Japanese culture...Bold, humorous and current. **Japan Society**

A delightful tumble into village life, complete with a vivid cast of characters and a beautiful sense of place. **The Scotsman**

Scottish writer Iain Maloney is far from home in this funny and uplifting read. Having decided to settle in a rural Japanese village, Iain and his wide imagine a world of pastoral delights – they meet bird-sized bees and hawk-eyed neighbours instead. **Wanderlust Magazine**

Laugh-out-loud lessons from Japan's proud countryside – layered with shrewd observations about race, gender and generation, and cultural asides, all glued together with levity and distinctive social commentary...a thought-provoking, lively examination of one immigrant's quest to create a new home outside his country of birth. **The Japan Times**

Maloney navigates culture shock, new hobbies and watchful neighbours, revealing in the process a rarely seen side of Japan.

Air Canada in-flight magazine

Praise for *In the Shadow of Piper Alpha*
(formerly *The Waves Burn Bright*)

My girlfriend's dad was one of the first salvage workers to get onto the Piper Alpha after the explosion. I saw the photographs one of his workmates secretly took of the devastation. In the Shadow of Piper Alpha is not just another, much needed representation of the human costs resulting from the unceasing and capricious chase for profits. It is also one which explores the long-term effects which go on behind the horrible headline of "167 killed".

**Gregor Gall, Visiting Professor of Industrial Relations
at the University of Leeds, editor *Scottish Left Review*,
director of the Jimmy Reid Foundation**

A cauldron of a book, bubbling with anger and magma which might at any moment spill over and bring further devastation. It is both particular to this tragedy in 1988, but also universal; a compelling story exploring how a father's trauma sends shock waves through a family, changes the pattern of lives – particularly his daughter's – and makes love risky. However, as well as being about damage and running away, it is also about healing.

**Linda Cracknell, author of
Doubling Back and *The Other Side of Stone***

A compelling and highly engaging story, told with insight and compassion, this novel deserves a wide readership.

Alison Miller, author of *Demo and Scots Scriever* for Orkney

The characters are well drawn and believable; the tortured survivor, struggling with dreams and the need to blot out memories with the bottle; the child damaged as much by the implosion of her parents' marriage as the disaster; and the guilt- ridden mother who has positioned herself outside the close unit of father and daughter but who still wants to revel in Carrie's achievements. The night of the disaster is sensitively and evocatively handled... Digging through a hard exterior to explore the layers beneath can be a dangerous and explosive exercise, whether that's the earth's crust or a human's weaker shell. In this novel both are explored in equally compelling ways.

The Scotsman

Other Books by Iain Maloney

Non-Fiction
The Only Gaijin in the Village

Fiction
In the Shadow of Piper Alpha (Formerly *The Waves Burn Bright*)
Life is Elsewhere/Burn Your Flags
Silma Hill
First Time Solo

Poetry
Envy the Seasons
(With Hamish Whyte and James McGonigal)
Fractures

As Editor
In the Empty Places

About the Author

Iain Maloney is the author of eight books, including the critically acclaimed *The Only Gaijin in the Village (Birlinn, 2020)*, a memoir about his life in rural Japan. He teaches creative writing and literature at Sugiyama Jogakuen University, and is also a freelance editor and journalist, mainly for *The Japan Times*. He was born and raised in Aberdeen, Scotland.

www.iainmaloney.substack.com
www.iainmaloney.com
On Twitter, Facebook and Instagram as Iain Maloney.

A Note on the Text

All Japanese names are written according to Japanese custom with family name first. There are many discrepancies in the spelling of place names when transliterated from Japanese script to romaji (Roman letters) such as Omaesaki/Omaezaki. In these instances I have sided with local usage. I have chosen to use Macrons (the bar above the vowel that indicates a long vowel such as ō and ū) even where they are customarily dropped. This is because while learning Japanese I find them incredibly useful as a guide to pronunciation and also because I think they make the black squiggles on the paper look prettier. I have undoubtedly made mistakes with the Japanese language for which I can only apologise.

For Minori

The Japan Lights

On The Trail of the Scot Who
Illuminated Japan's Coast

Iain Maloney

TIPPERMUIR
BOOKS LIMITED

The Japan Lights – Iain Maloney
Copyright © 2023. All rights reserved.

The right of Iain Maloney to be identified as the
author of the Work has been asserted in accordance with
the Copyright, Designs & Patents Act 1988.

This first edition published and copyright 2023 by
Tippermuir Books Ltd, Perth, Scotland.
mail@tippermuirbooks.co.uk – www.tippermuirbooks.co.uk.

ISBN 978-1-913836-32-0 (paperback).

A CIP catalogue record for this book is available
from the British Library.

Project coordination and editorial by Dr Paul S Philippou.
Cover design by Matthew Mackie.
Illustrations by Rob Hands.
Map by Bernard Chandler and Rob Hands

Editorial support:
Ajay Close, Steve Zajda and Jean Hands.

Text design, layout, and artwork by Bernard Chandler [graffik].
Text set in Garamond Pro 10.5/13pt with X titling.

Printed and bound by Ashford Colour Press, Gosport, PO13 0FW

Contents

Introduction

It was an epic road trip. I'd been travelling for about ten days, exploring Tōhoku, the northern part of Japan's main island. The area comprises six prefectures: Aomori, Iwate, Miyagi, Akita, Yamagata and Fukushima. I'd never been that far north and, having some free time on my hands, decided to throw the camping gear in the car and drift wherever my whims took me. Minori, my wife, came with me some of the way, spending a couple of nights in the mountains on the Nagano-Gunma border and a night in Niigata City. She flew home from there and I continued alone.

My Toyota Mark II Blit had 150,000 on the clock but was a dream to drive long distances: comfy, a great sound system, and with the seats down in the back there was more than two metres of space. More than once the thought of setting up the tent was too much and I simply unfolded my sleeping bag in the car. From Niigata I went west to Aizu-Wakamatsu, camping by a lake near the city, and then up the east coast.

I had two main goals for the trip. The first was to see this coast. Miyagi, Iwate and Fukushima were where the 2011 tsunami met Japan. Six years on, the area was still ravaged. Once fertile farmland was now barren, flooded and salted. Millions of planters stood on top of the fields, a bizarre sight, a sight of despair.

I was in Japan during that horrible period. I'd watched the tsunami roll across Tōhoku from the safety of my Aichi apartment more than 500 km away. I remember the tremors shaking our apartment that afternoon and watching the aftermath on TV. One broadcast showed the tsunami approaching a group of people fleeing for higher ground. At the back of the pack were an elderly couple, the husband struggling to help his wife. With the wave only a few metres from them he ran, abandoning her for a few steps before they were both engulfed. I don't think they ever repeated this broadcast.

We were watching NHK Japan on TV and NHK World on the

internet and listening to two directly contradictory news reports from the same network. In Japanese, everything was fine. In English, panic now.

Afterwards, I donated money. I wrote fiction and non-fiction about it. I thought about volunteering. Many people went to Tōhoku to volunteer, to help clearing, carrying, whatever they could. I didn't. I regret that. I feel guilty about that. Was it laziness, selfishness, fear of fallout? I still don't know. I just know I could have done more.

Now I wanted to see for myself. It took six years but I finally made my way to that coast. From Aizu-Wakamatsu I drove east and stopped in Minamisōma to use the laundrette and the public bath. Minamisōma is a nondescript Japanese town. Functional, pragmatic, not at all pretty, just another bog-standard Japanese town that also happens to be a few kilometres from the Fukushima exclusion zone. When I posted on Facebook that I was there, some friends told me I should leave as soon as possible.

The people were friendly, welcoming, but in a distant, reserved way. At the baths, the staff questioned me about tattoos in broken English, but when I replied in Japanese that I have none, they were all smiles. I was only there for a few hours but I felt an atmosphere, like a cloud hung over the place which, in a way, it did. These people would know people. These people would have lost people. For six years these people had been living in fear of symptoms, of sirens. How many sleepless nights? How many bad dreams?

I felt I was intruding. I had nothing to offer but a few yen into the economy. I paid for my bath, did my washing, I bought a few things at the local supermarket. The consumerist age when the act of shopping can be seen as 'helping'. What have we done to ourselves?

Up the coast. Brand new roads. Signs every few metres:

You are two metres above sea level.

Warning. Tsunami zone.

I was using Google Maps on my phone in lieu of satnav and it kept screaming to U-turn, U-turn, U-turn. These roads didn't exist. It hadn't updated to take into account the tarmac washed away, the new street plans.

As I drove north, I was struck most by the absence. The land is paper flat, the sea to my right, the mountains far, very, worryingly far to my left. Too far to reach in the event...The ground was flat and empty. Ripped flat, pounded flat, then cleared, scraped flat, scrubbed empty.

I stopped, climbed to the top of a tiny man-made hill. From there I could see a half-collapsed house, as yet not dealt with. Dumper trucks, diggers, yellow work machinery at the sides of roads or trundling across the landscape. Six years and reconstruction was still beginning. It brought to mind something a friend in Christchurch said about the 2011 earthquake there: 'After four years they've finally started putting up more than they're pulling down.'

I took a few photos but I was beginning to feel like maybe I was a disaster tourist. The people here had no need of me, I was not helping, I was not offering anything. I was just passing though. What would I say if someone spoke to me? How could I justify being there? I got back in the car and kept going, heading for the Miracle Pine in Iwate.

Out of 70,000 pine trees that once stood on this stretch of the Iwate coastline only one remained vertical, and it was dead. Paid for by donations, the tree had been reinforced and 'repaired', and now towered over the barren horizon, dwarfing the nearby municipal building bearing the marks of the sea, half caved in, air-conditioner units hanging from the walls, plaster and concrete flaking, stairs collapsed. One day this will be a memorial park, but that day it was just sad.

The next stop was Matsushima. Matsushima is officially one of Japan's three most beautiful views (the other two being Miyajima and Amanohashidate) and the pine-covered islands dotting the bay are picturesque but I was not in the mood. I was not in the mood for much. I was overwhelmed by emotion, by input. The view was obscured by row upon row of tourist restaurants, fading hotels, souvenir shops. Tourism in Japan doesn't know when to stop. When Bashō visited Matsushima, it was a stunning wilderness. Today it's shabby consumerism.

I asked at the tourist centre for a campsite. There were two but they were at least ninety minutes further up the coast. I was exhausted emotionally and physically but had little choice. I picked one and set off. It was dark by the time I arrived, got my tent up, and ate a Cup Ramen for dinner.

When I woke the next morning, I was still exhausted, utterly drained. I'd planned on taking the ferry to Kinkasan, a small island off the coast that is home to a lighthouse built by some Scotsman, but I couldn't find any information in Japanese or English about the ferry. The island was badly hit by the tsunami and it looked like it was discouraging visitors. I was in no position to argue. I packed up and went north to Hirosaki, where I booked a hotel.

I spent two nights in Hirosaki, only venturing out to find food. My enthusiasm for the trip had taken a battering. I lay in that cheap business hotel thinking about the sea, about death, and people.

My hometown, Aberdeen, was a fishing community before it became an oil town. The sea defines it. In a sense it defines me, though I'd only ever been slightly aware of the fact. I feel more centred, more grounded, when I'm near a body of water. With the sea at my back, I know where I am, where I'm going. Gifu, where I live, is far inland, one of very few landlocked prefectures in Japan. I have a constant low-level sense that something is missing.

I wrote and thought a lot about the sea in my novel, *In the Shadow of Piper Alpha*. It's about the Piper Alpha oil platform disaster, so the connection is unavoidable, but novels are black holes that suck all information and ideas into them. Disparate thoughts, things you've read, overheard, wondered about, all collide and fuse.

There's a scene in the *West Wing* where CJ is shown a map that reflects the actual size of the continents and it freaks her out. They then flip the map to show that north being at the top is only a cultural convention. Elsewhere, in a book by Jared Diamond I think, I read about how our conception of the coast as a boundary, the edge, the end, is only a modern affectation. Oceans were highways. If you were travelling from Aberdeen to Edinburgh for most of human history you'd go by sea: it was faster, safer, easier. The coastline wasn't the end, it was the beginning, the kerbstone, your front gate. Trains, cars, planes: we've lost this sense. I started imagining the map from this new perspective, maps that begin at the edge of land, from the north-east of Scotland, a road atlas of the deep. From Aberdeen, from this perspective, south becomes less relevant: east is the thing. The North Sea as a highway, a connection. Norway, Denmark, Sweden and Finland. I'd spent my life thinking everything was south of Aberdeen. Flip the map, shift the focus from land to sea, and there's a brave new world.

A character from *In the Shadow of Piper Alpha* gets these ideas. A minor character, but it's part of the tapestry of that novel and as time passes, it's one of the things that grows larger, keeps coming back to me. In Hirosaki those ideas returned. Unless our lives are directly connected - fishermen, merchant sailors, the Navy - we have turned our backs on the sea and faced inland. But the sea didn't go anywhere and every once in a while, it taps us on the shoulder, reminds us of our precarious position on the dry twenty-nine percent of the planet.

Writing *The Only Gaijin in the Village* also churned these ideas as I tried to make sense of how I'd gone from a commuter town outside Aberdeen to a rural community in Japan. That book was an attempt to explain to myself who I was and why I felt more comfortable in Japan than in Scotland. Doing so involved pulling on a lot of these threads, one of which was the great history of migration, of exiles, the differences between expats and immigrants, between those who move because they want to and those who move because they can. As with all the books I have written, it ended up raising more questions than it answered.

While I lay in that Hirosaki hotel room exhausted by my tardy confrontation with mortality, the other thing I did was to read more about this Scotsman who built a lighthouse on Kinkasan.

I'd come across Brunton years before. In 2009, on a visit to Yokohama, I found myself wandering through the Foreign Cemetery. Yokohama was the first full foreign settlement on Japanese soil after 250 years of Sakoku (self-enforced isolation). The island of Dejima at Nagasaki had held a Dutch settlement but that was very deliberately kept separate from the mainland by gates and armed guards. After US gunboat diplomacy (begun in 1853) opened Japan to world trade, Yokohama became the main foreign settlement. Yokohama is central to Brunton's story, so we'll return to one of my favourite Japanese towns later. For now, let's stay in the graveyard.

As an adolescent I had an affinity with graveyards, finding them peaceful, secluded, beautiful. Some of my worst teenage poetry was on this theme, so I was naturally drawn into the gates to stroll amongst the ageing stones and well-tended foliage. On The Bluff, a later addition to the foreign settlement in Yokohama, open to a dramatic view, the cemetery's first guest was Robert Williams, a member of Perry's crew (the first US ships to arrive in Japan), though his body was later moved. The prize for longest lying goes to two Russians, Roman Mophet and Ivan Sokoloff, murdered by Nationalists in 1859.

Walking around, four years into my own life in Japan, I was struck by the parallels. I've written stories set in the sixteenth century, the eighteenth century, in World War Two, in the future, in multiple countries, on other planets, and one thing I've learned from this is that people are people. As humans we haven't changed all that much. Certainly not over a couple of centuries. The technology has changed. Our ways of talking about ourselves and the world has changed. But what drives us, what moves us, what matters, that hasn't changed. Take John Diack, another resident of the Foreign Cemetery, a railway engineer. 150 years before I stood beside his grave, he too travelled from Aberdeen to Yokohama and made his home - his eternal home, it turned out - there.

It was comforting, making me feel less alone, less ground-breaking, less like a pioneer. I was just another in a long line of Scotsmen who'd left home seeking...what? A new life, a better life, a life less ordinary, seeking something anyway. One reason I've always liked learning about history is that those big sweeps of time make sense, those oceans of generations moving, building, progressing, failing, falling back, trying again. That apocryphal story about Zhou Enlai saying 200 years was too soon to assess the impact of the French Revolution; when I first read that it was one of those epiphany moments, when something you've pondered is defined, named, shared. Our lifetimes are short; history is long. On a long enough timeline, anything is possible. We're part of a chain that will end somewhere and from above, from a distance, life looks good. The macro works for me, gives me perspective. It's the micro that's problematic. I can comprehend millennia; the next seven days, that's unsettling.

Writing is how I process life. Input becomes output. I got an article out of that trip, and it sparked a curiosity that led to more writing. I first met Richard Henry Brunton while looking around for more articles to write. I wrote a piece on Thomas Glover, the 'Scottish Samurai' from Fraserburgh who came to Japan in 1859. Glover was, as Alan Spence proved in his novel *The Pure Land*, a character. He had a finger in every pie, went bankrupt a number of times, helped start Mitsubishi and Kirin Beer, once imported a train to demonstrate the technology, ran guns for the Chōshū rebels, helped smuggle Chōshū and Satsuma men out of Japan, had a hand in building the dry dock at Nagasaki with equipment imported from Aberdeen that is still there today. He is perhaps most bizarrely remembered on labels of Kirin beer, where his moustache adorns the kirin, a mythical Japanese beast.

I wrote another about Rita Cowan from Kirkintilloch, who married Taketsuru Masataka in 1920, and together they brought whisky distilling to Japan. One possible stop on this trip was Yoichi, where they built their distillery. It made me curious to discover other Scots who had made the same journey.

There are plenty. For a small nation we get about. Yokohama's Foreign General Cemetery is packed with Scots, but the one who grabbed my attention wasn't in that cemetery, rather he's buried in West Norwood Cemetery in London: Richard Henry Brunton.

In 1868, Japan underwent a revolution. It was a top-down revolution led by elite members of society who felt themselves excluded from a status quo that had lasted for two-and-a-half centuries, but a revolution nonetheless. Seemingly overnight Japan moved from feudalism to modern industrial capitalism. To facilitate this, the new Japanese government hired o-yatoi-gaikokujin, foreign experts to guide and teach a first generation of Japanese lawyers, bankers, architects, military leaders: pretty much every part of society including, of course, civil engineering. The Tom Cruise film *The Last Samurai* however flawed (and it is) is based on this process.

With increased international trade, Japan's island-strewn coastal waters had to be made safe for international shipping. Lighthouses were needed, and fast. The French won the contract and began work, but the British government, by no means unbiased in their opinion, argued that the French were taking too long. Sir Harry Parkes - a name that comes up again and again in this period, and one we will be returning to later on - persuaded the Japanese government that the Stevensons were the very men for this job. David and Thomas Stevenson, the third generation of the Lighthouse Stevensons, as Bella Bathurst named them, (Thomas being father of Robert Louis Stevenson) were the pre-eminent engineers of the day. The Stevensons began the search for a chief engineer and hit upon Brunton as the man who would travel to Japan and do for the emergent nation what the Stevensons had done for Scotland: *light it up.*

Between 1868 and 1876, Brunton built lighthouses, supplemented by buoys, beacons and lightships, constructed the first iron bridge in the country, planned the streets, sewage system and gas lighting of Yokohama, erected their first telegraph system, and helped establish the first railway, all in a country so beset by earthquakes that many of the basic 'Western' assumptions about engineering had to be rethought. He also found time to father a second daughter and irritate his Japanese employers so much that in 1876 he found his services were no longer required.

He returned to Britain where he slipped into obscurity, dying in 1901. He wrote up an account of his travels which remained effectively unpublished until 1991, the 150th anniversary of his birth.

It's not a great book. You can see why no one published it for 150 years and why it then slipped back out of print. What Brunton did is fascinating. What he said about what he did, isn't. Engineers don't always make good writers. Robert Louis Stevenson famously had to choose, one or the other. You couldn't be both, not in those days. Brunton was a great engineer but a mediocre writer. But it's not just how he writes, it's also what he says. His views haven't aged well. By the standards of his time his opinions on the 'other races' are not that surprising, but Brunton was also haughty, arrogant and stubborn. He doesn't come across well. No argument can be made for renewed publication of his memoirs or for a rehabilitation of his character, and I attempt neither here. Nevertheless, there is a statue of him in Yokohama Park, and it is right that there should be. He is not raised onto that plinth because he was a likeable man. He's there because of what he did to transform Yokohama and to make Japanese waters safe.

Initially, a few words in the potted biography on Wikipedia stood out, those initial tendrils of a story. Muchalls is only a few miles south of Aberdeen and I know it well. He had links with the Iwakura Mission, one of the events in Japanese history with which I am most fascinated. He left Japan in 1876 after a disagreement with Japanese officials. That last part. The fact of it, the way it's described. A disagreement. It leaves a lot of questions unanswered, always tempting for a writer. It also hints at a personality. Was he the cause of the disagreement? Was he a troublemaker or did he reach the end of his patience with Japanese bureaucracy? Maybe it was me reading too much into a simple sentence but I felt I could detect a mischievous character behind the words. Whatever, there was a window into a life that intrigued me.

According to Wikipedia, twenty-six of his lighthouses still stand, though four of those have been extinguished. The idea that came to me as I regrouped in Hirosaki was simple: I would travel around Japan, visiting them all, and write about it.

Initially, I wanted to do it in one go. I'm a fan of travel books like *Round Ireland with a Fridge* and random mission narratives like *Are You Dave Gorman?* (showing my age here with these pop culture references). Unfortunately, I wasn't in a position, financially, to take the time off work and spend the money to do it all in one trip. Lighthouses are, necessarily, in out of the way, difficult to reach places. But I could still visit as many as logistically possible and my trip to Tōhoku was my chance to test the idea. I'd travel to Shiriyazaki in Aomori, the same prefecture as Hirosaki, one of the most out of the way lighthouses on the list and then, on the way home, try again for Kinkasan. After driving around aimlessly writing haiku about desolation, I now had a purpose.

1　Shiriyazaki Lighthouse
2　Wadamisaki Lighthouse
3　Esaki Lighthouse
4　Anorisaki Lighthouse
5　Sugashima Lighthouse
6　Kashinozaki Lighthouse
7　Shionomisaki Lighthouse
8　Tomogashima Lighthouse
9　Omaezaki Lighthouse
10　Inubōsaki Lighthouse
11　Nabeshima Lighthouse
12　Nosappumisaki Lighthouse
13　Irōzaki Lighthouse
14　Tsunoshima Lighthouse
15　Mutsurejima Lighthouse
16　Shirasu Lighthouse

17　Hesaki Lighthouse
18　Eboshijima Lighthouse
19　Iojima Lighthouse
20　Satamisaki Lighthouse
21　Frank Lake Grave
22　Tsurushima Lighthouse
23　Tsurugisaki Lighthouse
24　Mikomotoshima Lighthouse
25　Kinkasan Lighthouse
26　Onagawa

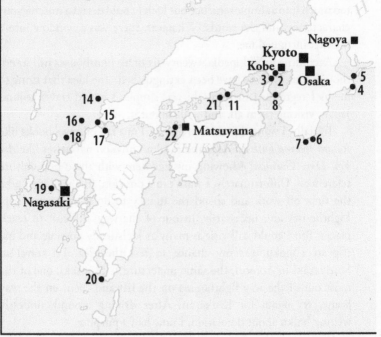

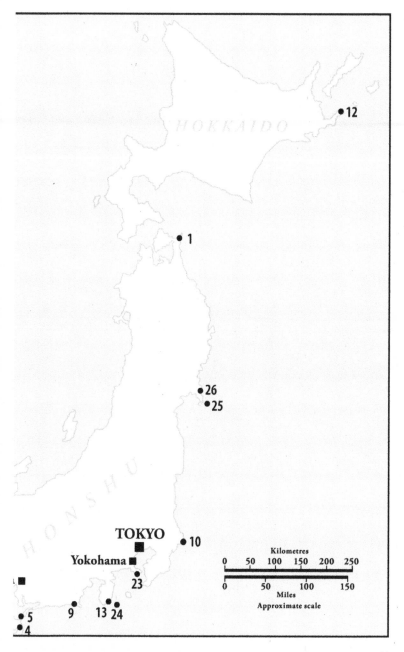

HOKKAIDO

● 12

● 1

● 26
● 25

HONSHU

TOKYO ■
● 10

Yokohama ■

● 23

■

● 5   ● 9   ● 13 ● 24

● 4

Kilometres

0   50   100   150   200   250

0   50   100   150
Miles
Approximate scale

1. *Shiriyazaki Lighthouse*

With my new-found motivation I'm up early and back on the road. I make it to Shiriyazaki mid-morning, a four-hour drive through beautiful countryside right to the most north-eastern tip of Honshū, Japan's main island. The area is isolated, a spit of land in the freezing northern Pacific. The other horn of Aomori is misty on the western horizon. This place is wild, almost abandoned, forgotten, but important, a loop in the string that binds Japan. Outside the whitewashed and generally well-tended walls the land is given over for grazing something: just what isn't immediately clear but the piles of shit suggest a large mammal of some kind. Smaller creatures are also evident. Signs warn of ticks and bites. Behind, on an outcrop, wind turbines churn. A lot of Aomori has been given over to energy production - solar panels, thousands of turbines and nuclear waste storage. Nimbyism clearly isn't prevalent in northern Aomori.

Shiriyazaki is about what you'd expect of a lighthouse - tall, cylindrical, a bit worn and grubby. Boxy at the base. Steps leading up to bolted and chained metal doors - this is a working lighthouse with no museum, though it is obviously an acknowledged tourist destination. Plaques, explanations and a souvenir shop attest to that. It occasionally opens to the public but so rarely that there is no permanent ticket booth. I assumed I'd be the only person here but it's gratifyingly busy. Eight cars on an overcast Monday morning beyond the end of the summer holidays. Elderly couples mostly, one lone woman in her forties, two men in company overalls presumably taking a detour on a business trip. What looks like a hiking trail leads off behind the small café and gift shop and a local bus has been by twice already, depositing hikers. I'm surprised to see other people; they are surprised to see a foreigner.

Shiriyazaki was illuminated on 20 October 1876 (Meiji 9 in the Japanese calendar), making it one of Brunton's later lighthouses. It is 7.2 m in diameter at the base and stands 33 m tall making it, apparently, the tallest brick tower in Japan. I'm told the brick is 'British' but it's unclear whether than means actually imported from Britain (it's possible it was salvaged from ballast) or made according to British specifications. Brunton, as we'll see, was dismissive of most Japanese techniques but was also a pragmatist working on a budget.

The air is full of the clang of rope against the twin flagpoles, both empty. I like to think that once they flew Japan's national flag, the Hinomaru, and the Saltire, but there's no chance the Japanese would have flown a foreign flag up here. Anyway, back then it would have been the Union Flag. Was Brunton a Brit or a Scot first? Does that question even make sense for Victorians? Is it a modern assumption of identity I'm projecting back?

Gazing up at the tower, I wonder how much time Brunton spent here, if any. Did he come to survey? Was he here for the breaking of the ground? Or did he delegate?

These questions can only be a good sign for a writer: my subject has depth and breadth. There are places to go, a chain to follow. I sense, here on the tip of Aomori, at the end of land, at the beginning of the ocean, the threads of a story. At this point it's only that, the faint glimmer of a light on the horizon, a direction, nothing more.

The souvenir shop opens. Everyone but me departs. I feel extremely comfortable here, at ease for the first time in days. I take photos, wander around, down to the water on both sides, offer a little prayer at the shrine, more out of respect than anything, I don't know these gods and they don't know me. I pick up a sliver of red brick that has come off the wall, a souvenir, something tangible, tactile, part of the structure. In the shop I buy a keyring and some coffee, chat briefly to the woman working there. The grazing animals, it turns out, are horses. She gestures vaguely up the hill when I ask where they are. They are horses. They'll be wherever they feel like being.

On the way back south, making for Kinkasan and my second lighthouse, I stop for the night at Hachinohe. In the small hours my idyllic lakeside campsite is invaded by Bōsōzoku, a biker gang with links to the yakuza. I watch them rev their engines, do donuts, bored kids looking for a way to kill time. I'm the only other person here, even the staff have gone home for the night. I don't want to be their way of killing time. I quietly pack the tent into the car and drive off. Starting the engine and turning on the headlights alerts them to my presence and instantly they are after me, a buzz of swerving lights in the rear-view mirror. I put my foot down, make it onto the highway and pull in at the first service station, spend the rest of the night there. The morning after, North Korea tests a missile overhead and I turn straight for home. Kinkasan can wait.

2. *Brunton Before Japan*

Richard Henry Brunton - he went by Henry - was born in Muchalls, Kincardineshire, on 26 December 1841, to Richard Brunton and Margaret Telfer. Muchalls is on the east coast of Scotland between Aberdeen and Stonehaven. A North-east laddie, like me. Some sources give his birthplace as Fetteresso, but this seems to be a confusion of villages in close proximity to one another as well as a confusion of siblings. His sister Mary Louisa was born in Fetteresso on 14 July 1843, suggesting a flit at some point between the births of the first and second child as space became paramount.

His father was in the Royal Navy (sources give his rank variously as captain and lieutenant, though if he was a captain, he may first have been a lieutenant) but came from a theatrical family. His great-grandfather and grandfather were both actors and theatre managers in England. His great-grandfather, John Brunton, played Hamlet at Covent Garden in 1774. His great aunts also cracked the boards, as did his aunt Elizabeth and her husband, Fredrick Henry Yates. They seem to have been quite the theatrical dynasty. One of his grandfather's acting sisters, Louisa - most famous for her Beatrice in *Much Ado About Nothing* - married Count William Craven, becoming Countess of Craven. Quite why Brunton's father joined the Royal Navy when the rest of his family took to the stage is unknown, but there's a nice mirroring here of the Stevenson family, who were exclusively engineers apart from Robert Louis, who preferred the arts. The fact that Louisa's name became Brunton's sister Mary's middle name suggests the two branches of the family - the Scottish maritime pragmatics and the English theatrical artists - hadn't completely split from each other. One can easily imagine having a countess in the family carrying quite the social cachet in rural Victorian Scotland. Towards the end of Brunton's life the journey came full circle when he was involved in designing the Palace of Varieties in Cork and in redesigning what is now the

Olympia Theatre in Dublin.

He was privately educated before beginning his engineering training in Aberdeen in 1856 at the age of fifteen with P D Brown. He completed his apprenticeship under John Willet, also in Aberdeen, in 1860. Willet subsequently took him on as an assistant. Willet was a celebrated engineer and architect who at that time worked out of an office at 123 Union Street in the heart of the city. He later moved to Union Terrace. Today, 123 Union Street is depressingly a Taco Bell. Born in Ayrshire in 1815, his career took him all over the country but Aberdeen became his permanent home after he married local quine Mary Ann Rennie in 1854. Willet's area of expertise was bridges, which pulled him into the nineteenth-century railway boom. He worked on lines in England and Scotland and is responsible for many bridges across Scotland and harbour works up and down the north-east coastline. John and Mary were buried in Allenvale Cemetery, Aberdeen, a peaceful, picturesque graveyard beside Duthie Park, on the north bank of the River Dee filled with busts of Victorian men and enough stone angels to terrify any *Doctor Who* fan.

While with Willet, Brunton worked on railway projects including the Forfar to Dundee railway line, the Ballater extension and the Denburn Valley Line. He worked under the supervision of John and Allen Grainger on the Ross-shire extension in 1863, for which he received a reference describing him as 'a very competent person...active, laborious & perfectly sober'. Laborious presumably had a more positive meaning in 1863. He also took part in work that would prepare him for what was to come in Japan, including planning a reservoir, conducting a survey of the River Dee and 'in setting out & looking after the works of the drainage of the Old Town of Aberdeen' (according to Willet's 1864 letter of reference).

In October 1864 Brunton left Willet's employment for that of William Robert Galbraith and Julian Horne Tolme in London. His six years with Willet clearly gave him an impressive resumé and reputation, with both Willet and the Graingers expressing disappointment at losing 'a most valuable assistant'. Brunton was with Galbraith and Tolme for less than a year, working on the

London and South West Railway. In August 1865 he took a position with Henry Bolen of the Barry Railway and Harbour Company, based in Westminster, though much of Brunton's work was in Wales and along the south coast.

One can imagine the ambitious young man of twenty-three years from rural Aberdeenshire heading off for the smoke and bustle of the capital. He had already travelled extensively in Scotland but this was, as far as we know, his first time down south. From the age of fifteen he had been moving away from home, and this was the next big step. There is no record of Brunton's thought processes at this time, whether he was anxious or excited, blasé or reluctant, but everything written about him suggests a strong character, a man of confidence and energy. He may well have been planning the move for years, or he may have seized an opportunity as it arose. The short stint with Galbraith certainly suggests a streak of opportunism, though Bolden's 1867 letter of reference says that he had known 'Mr Henry Brunton' for ten years. Presumably they met in 1858 when Bolden worked with the Scottish Central Railway. Brunton was making connections and building his reputation from an early age. It would be this that landed him the Japan lighthouse job in 1868.

Bolden's letter of reference is both effusive and detailed. He begins by stressing his 'high moral character' before mentioning that he is 'extremely temperate both in his habits and temper'; the second time his sobriety was raised, clearly an issue for the buttoned-up Victorians or maybe just countering stereotypes of Scots. Bolden discusses both the difficult nature of the work Brunton has undertaken and the flawless way it was executed. The letter is shot through with personal affection and a powerful desire for Brunton to get the lighthouse job. While the comment about his temper doesn't gel with later impressions and Brunton's own accounts of the frustrations of working in Japan, it's clear that Brunton was popular and respected by his professional peers.

It was while working with Bolden that Brunton married Elizabeth Charlotte Wauchope from Bonnington, Edinburgh, known as Eliza. Not much is known about Eliza's background, or how the couple met, but the *Oxford Dictionary of National Biography* says her father was a clerk for the North British Railway Company, which would certainly put him and Brunton in the same social circle. Their marriage banns were posted 'on three several Sundays' at St Martin-in-the-Fields church where Brunton was 'a member of this parish'. They were married in Middlesex on 22 December 1865, when Brunton was twenty-four and Eliza was twenty-two. (The *Oxford Dictionary of National Biography* places their wedding in Edinburgh, but a book on Brunton produced by the Yokohama Archives of History reproduces the marriage certificate clearly stating St Martin-in-the-Fields.) Two years later their first child, Mary Elizabeth, was born.

At the start of 1868 Brunton applied for a post in India but was unsuccessful. At the same time, Sir Harry Parkes, Her Majesty's Envoy Extraordinary and Minister Plenipotentiary and Consul-General in Japan, turned to the Stevensons to help Japan meet its treaty obligations and make international shipping in Japanese waters safe. Brunton applied and on 24 February he was offered this job 'travelling to Japan to build lighthouses and train Japanese to operate them [and] building or improving roads and drainage in the foreign settlements of the treaty ports'. He was to be hired directly by the Japanese government, the chief engineer for a whole series of massive civil engineering works. He relocated to Edinburgh for a crash course in lighthouse engineering from the world experts in the subject, and it's a credit to his talent and hard work that it only took a few months to get him up to speed and give him such a good grasp of the subject that he could later improvise and adapt to meet the needs of the Japanese situation.

Two assistants were hired to accompany Brunton. The first was Hebridean Colin Alexander McVean, three years Brunton's senior and just as qualified. McVean later stated that he would have applied for the top job if he'd known about it in time. This rivalry would cause problems between him and Brunton later. His experience involved maritime surveys of the Hebrides and railway work in Bulgaria. The other was Archibald Woodward Blundell, about whom little is known.

In April 1868 Willet nominated him for associate membership

of the Institute of Civil Engineers. His training was over. All his hard work and networking had come to fruition. His reputation and glowing references had landed him the job that would define him. His young family packed up their life and on 13 June 1868, joined by Eliza's elder sister Mary, Brunton's two new assistants, and Blundell's wife, Mary, set sail aboard the SS Aden.

A photograph from this time beams confidence. He is standing, leaning jauntily on the edge of a lectern upon which his top hat rests, upturned. He is wearing a tailored suit, coat with tails, waistcoat, chain from a pocket watch, holding a long umbrella. Here is an upwardly mobile Victorian gentleman ready to take on the world. His hair is short, combed into a side parting, perhaps blonde though the photo is monochrome. His face is boyish, puckish almost, despite the massive mutton chop sideburns. It was this photo that first attracted me to Brunton as a subject – his face belies a mixture of characteristics: serious, ambitious, young, humorous, perhaps even mischievous. As he looks off camera into the distance, is that a hint of fear? Nerves? Life so far has been good to Henry Brunton, his career and family are both going well, and now his future opens before him on the other side of the world. A penny for his thoughts on that day.

3. *An Aside on the Character of the Man*

There's a BBC Radio 4 programme, *Great Lives*, where notable people nominate figures from history who they feel have lived the titular great life. The host, Matthew Parris, along with an expert - usually a biographer - discuss the highs and lows of the nominee's time on the planet and decide if their life was, in fact, great.

It's never quite clear what a great life actually is. Terms are never defined. Does great equal good, as in the modern usage? Does it mean important, notable, as in Alexander the Great? Or perhaps it just means big, encompassing, as in Great Britain. Lytton Strachey chose his words carefully when naming his *Eminent Victorians*. Not *Great Victorians*. Not good Victorians, or large Victorians, just ones you'd have heard of. Ones that stood out from the crowd. The nails who stuck out, to paraphrase a Japanese proverb.

When we talk of a great life today, we tend to mean good. Moral. Ethical. Objectively, justifiably good. We don't like nuance, we don't like contradiction, not in our heroes, and the assumption is that if you are examining a life, you are suggesting it is worthy of emulation. A role model. Someone you'd want your kids to look up to. You don't want to recommend your child follows in the footsteps of someone who produced great art while committing sins of the flesh, or who bestrode the world like a colossus while oppressing one community or another, or who professed charity and humbleness while showing none in their private life. That's fair enough. The ancient Egyptians believed that in the afterlife you had to weigh your heart against a feather. Sin is a sliding scale. No one is blameless; there is always a reckoning.

But how light is our feather today? Do we expect too much, demand a purity that is fantastical? Where does this leave us? Who should we study? If we only learn about the good, the perfect, and excise the rest then our books are going to be thin and our mistakes frequent. Who is truly good? Even saints aren't, not really. Churchill,

Mother Theresa, Gandhi, depending on your perspective, they all have their flipside, their other hand. No one's life holds up to examination if all you are looking for is perfection.

I write this at a time when there is a lot of discussion around the world about how we engage with the figures of history and their views. Einstein's travel diary, long available to scholars, was made public to media outcry at what *The Guardian* called the 'shocking xenophobia' displayed in his comments about the Chinese, who he described as 'industrious, filthy, obtuse people'. While what Einstein wrote is objectively awful by any stands, the tone of much of the 'Western' coverage was over the top, seemingly implying that now Einstein's true character had been revealed, who even knew anymore what 'E' might equal. Japanese media focused on the part where Einstein compared them favourably to their continental neighbours. In China, ironically, the *South China Morning Post* defended Einstein, describing his private words as part of a 'self-conversation,' while social media users in China apparently went so far as to admit Einstein had a point - he was talking about China pre-Communist revolution and his comments were spun to show how far China has come and how successful the revolution has been.

But there is a serious point behind it, a deadly serious one as scenes in Charlottesville in the summer of 2017 demonstrated and as fractious statements about the statue of Cecil Rhodes at Oriel College, Oxford, showed. How do we deal with the past from our modern stand point? Good people do bad things. We all make statements at one point in our lives that we would disown at a later time, part of our 'self-conversation' as we develop intellectually. Should one diary entry, tweet or drunken outburst define a multi-decade life? At the same time, and with reference to Rhodes, should we literally raise up someone who consistently championed causes and ideologies that today are criminal and reprehensible. To acknowledge fault is not to 're-write history,' it is to contextualise and explore. Statues aren't eternal and, as the British Museum clearly shows, can easily be relocated and re-contextualised, assuming you have the imperial network to manage the logistics. Simply smashing the statue, tearing it down like the US Army did with Saddam

Hussein's, won't deal with the issue. Why not move the statues to a museum where all sides of the story can be told?

We, especially in Britain, but more widely around the world, need to find a way to talk honestly about the past without getting weighed down by ideology. Saying, 'it was a different time, things were done differently then', doesn't help, but neither does no-platforming or cancelling. In Ian Buruma's excellent book *Wages of Guilt* he examines the different reactions to loss in World War Two by Japan and Germany, and the consequences of those reactions today. He concludes, convincingly, that sweeping it all under the rug helps no one.

Throughout his memoir Brunton displays both a high opinion of himself and his 'civilisation'. He comes across badly in his own words, and in the words of others. It would be easy to dismiss Brunton's tone and comments about his Japanese hosts as 'normal for his era' but when laid alongside those of contemporaries like Sir Ernest Satow, a British diplomat who came to Japan in 1862 as a student interpreter, we see a sharp contrast.

Brunton openly mocks Japanese men who were understandably nonplussed on encountering 'catsup' for the first time. This is childish point-scoring whichever age you are from. I once watched a Japanese TV programme whose main purpose seemed to be laughing at people in rural Africa who couldn't name the members of Japanese pop groups. It isn't acceptable now and it wasn't acceptable then.

Satow's own memoir, *A Diplomat in Japan*, manages a more balanced tone, highlighting good and bad on both sides of the cultural encounter. Brunton arrived in Japan less than a decade after On the Origin of Species was published and only thirty-five years on from the death of William Wilberforce. To say there was a consensus on attitudes to race and other nationalities is a gross oversimplification. Sure, these were the dark days before political correctness when expression of prejudice was more mainstream, but that doesn't mean the prejudice was shared by all.

So how to deal with Brunton's imperial, colonial condescension while writing a book about him? By writing about Brunton, I am not raising him up as someone to emulate, but I am also arguing that he shouldn't be forgotten by history. Neil Pedlar writes in *Imported Pioneers*, his book on the O-yatoi-gaikokujin that:

> The reason why hardly any of them are well-known in the West and only partly appreciated in Japan, except to a few history students, is that their lives had little nationalistic significance. The heroes who are publicised and popularised in various countries are those who took part in destructive activities abroad. Those who crossed national barriers to perform constructive tasks tended to be ignored because their own leaders did not want their people to admire a person whose education was more advanced in some field, who had a strange appearance and ways, for it could have been taken as a reflection of that country's incompetence and inferiority. The country of emigration, delighted on the one hand that one of its subjects may influence other people, on the other hand ignores and distrusts such men in case they bring back new and 'foreign' ideas to upset the status quo.

Brunton made a significant contribution, a contribution that continues to be important today as evidenced by those lighthouses still protecting shipping 150 years later. I can't ignore the way he writes about the people he encounters, his xenophobia, his racism, his condescending tone and haughty patriarchal superiority, but nor can I condemn him out of hand as someone to be forgotten. His contribution deserves to be remembered.

From the beginning of this project, of learning more about Brunton, his time and his experiences, it has felt like a conversation, even though it may be a self-conversation with an imagined Brunton. I feel like if I'd been there in Yokohama with him and a decent whisky, we could've had a damn good argument about the whole thing but that's the point, isn't it? We can't. We have to have both sides of the conversation without allowing bias to slip in. Oh, for a night on the whisky with these men, Brunton, Glover, Satow, Parkes. Would I come away with more questions than answers? Probably. That seems to be how I go through life. Questions are always more important than answers. Maybe the point is that there are no heroes, if we take a hero to be someone that we would want to emulate in every way. If so, I'm happy with that. No more heroes, no more villains, just flawed, messy, broken humans. The Japanese art of kintsugi, where broken pottery is mended with gold that highlights the cracks resonates with artists around the world because it so beautifully reflects our essential selves: fractured but holding it together.

On the other hand, context is important. Brunton crops up in other people's accounts of their time in Japan and most have nothing but praise for his work. I say most, because Brunton clearly had a 'suffer no fools' attitude. He was a frequent writer of letters to 'The Editor' and didn't hold back when he disagreed with someone. In the back of one version of his memoir, the editor has reproduced a war of words with another Scottish engineer Henry Dyer, that took place across the letters pages of *The Japan Weekly News*. In the Yokohama Archives I found evidence of others. William Elliot Griffis, an American who bought Brunton's manuscript and heavily edited it, writes in his 1906 introduction that Brunton's:

> own pronounced limitations appear in his own story and need not be enlarged on. He was a man of conscience who was impatient with anything but good work. He may have been a severe disciplinarian, but that was what both his employers and workmen needed.

In many ways Brunton was exactly the Victorian man you'd imagine, from hat and whiskers to imperial bluster. He was a man of principles, unwilling – maybe even unable – to compromise. He was difficult to work for and difficult to manage. Reading his memoir and what others have written, he comes across at times as determined, obstinate, intolerant, impatient, arrogant, energetic, conscientious, courageous and touchy. In his eight years in Japan, he had at least fifteen supervisors, and it can only be imagined what they thought of this foreigner who refused to follow Japanese officialdom's strong sense of hierarchy and the respect due to superiors. He was aware of this but saw it as his duty to see the job done properly and to the best of his ability and so felt that 'at whatever personal discomfort or self-sacrifice, I should assert my position as the responsible conductor of operations'. In other words, he set himself on a direct collision course with Japanese bureaucracy, and while he won many battles, there was only ever going to be one victor in the end.

He had a vision, and a good sense of what needed to be done, and the skills and motivation to achieve this. He was an ideal yatoi, an artisan hired to do a job, rather than one of the entrepreneurs Satow writes of who flooded into Yokohama after the opening. He wasn't in Japan to get rich - his contract saw to that - but the possibilities were there. Glover had come to Japan to do a job and quickly struck out on his own, gaining and losing more than one fortune in the process. Brunton was a different man, not a wanderer, not an adventurer, though he wasn't afraid of travel or of trying something new. When his job was done, he returned to Britain and got to work there. He died at fifty-nine, and Japan was but an eight-year interlude.

Brunton was a man 'of a thoroughly practical mind and well-trained for his future work' according to Griffis, who knew Brunton while in Japan. Yet he came from an artistic family, perhaps the mirror of Stevenson, the writer from a family of engineers. As Griffis points out, Brunton's father was 'a writer of sea-stories', his cousin was Edmund Yates, a journalist, editor and prolific novelist who worked with Dickens, and the family had numerous connections to the theatre. Whether Brunton and his family attended the Gaiety Theatre in Yokohama which opened in 1870 is unknown, though given the paucity of 'honest' amusement in the settlement (sports and horse racing being your lot) it would be a safe assumption that Eliza and Mary would have been keen on the entertainment.

He certainly had a sense of humour of the dry, sarcastic Scottish kind. Commenting upon efforts to open the Port of Osaka 'nullified' by the discovery of a sand bar across the entrance, he wryly stated that, 'Nature seemed to have been victorious over diplomacy'. Parkes, a man apparently universally popular, in turn appears to have been fond of Brunton. A part of their correspondence is reproduced by

Brunton and the tone of the letters is one of mutual respect and a certain informality behind the Victorian register.

In short, Brunton appears to have been entirely human, a man who was respected by many, liked by some. Nevertheless, chapters like 'The Jealous Japanese', 'The Japanese In Bad Temper' and 'Personal Judgements' make for unpalatable and sometimes nauseating reading.

History is not about finding role models, it's about learning what happened before, good and bad. It's perhaps more important to learn about the flawed, the failed, the bad eggs in all their sulphuric glory. What can you learn from a saint? That it takes a papal decree and centuries of whitewashing to build a flawless resumé? No, we learn about the eminent and the rest, because we are all eminent, from a certain angle, in a certain light.

Richard Henry Brunton had a great life, in the Strachey sense. Eminent. This book is pretty much making that argument, in a roundabout, tangential kind of way. Not a good life - there was much about Brunton that wasn't good, certainly not to be emulated, not least his way of treating others, and his attitude to his Japanese employers and employees - but what he achieved, his legacy, that is undeniably great. Brunton has already been forgotten by history, in his native Scotland at least if not in Japan, but his sins don't warrant permanent erasure. His work deserves to be remembered, celebrated, even if few of us would invite him for a pint after that work was done. Because of Brunton, countless lives have been saved. That's pretty great in my book.

4. *Wadamisaki and Esaki Lighthouses*

Kansai is officially 'western Japan'. Says so right there in the kanji. It isn't. Neither is it 'all Japan outside Tōkyō' as one American Tōkyōite told me. Chūbu, where I live, is the heart (the first character of Chūbu means centre). Kansai is west of that, but there's a hell of a lot of Japan after Kansai. Literally acres of it. Kansai is just off-centre. Centre-left as the map lies.

The literary translator Louise Heal Kawai has suggested that if Tōkyō is the London of Japan, then Osaka is Manchester. In many ways the analogy holds up, and her translation of part of Kawakami Mieko's *Breasts and Eggs for Words Without Borders* into Mancunian is delightful, a triumph of the translator's art. However, I would counter that Glasgow is a closer comparison. The second city of the empire, working class and fiercely proud of it, the industrial heart of the nation and home to an incomprehensible people who proclaim themselves welcoming and hilarious despite all evidence to the contrary. People who insist on being welcoming and hilarious to a point way beyond what is either welcoming or hilarious.

Osaka is the hub of Kansai, and Kyōto the tourist target, but for me it's Kōbe that is the gem of Kansai. Humbler than Kyōto, less brash than Osaka, a city forever scarred by the Great Hanshin Earthquake that killed somewhere between 5,500 and 6,500 people. A small strip of city cast between the mountains and the sea, a city slowly pushing its way over reclaimed land into the Pacific, a city of art, jazz and cosmopolitanism.

To the north the hills rise sharply, dotted with cable cars, restaurants, temples, roofs breaking the tree line. My father and I have an ongoing in-joke that anywhere we go, *looks just like Scotland*. A lot of the world does. It was a joke shamelessly stolen by Ewan McGregor and Charley Boorman in their *Long Way Round* TV show where they regularly noted that vast swathes of eastern Europe, Russia and the former Soviet Union looked just like Scotland.

Japan can, on occasion, but when I first arrived here in 2005, I was more struck by how little it looked like Scotland. I cite the hills as Exhibit A. Geologically, Scotland is much older, ergo the hills are smaller, rounded down by millennia of wind, rain, landslides and trampling feet, hoofs and paws. Japan's hills retain their birthmarks, the sharp, jagged peaks created by tectonic plates crashing into each other, a soft, flaky surface prone to slippage. The landscape is also marked by rice production. Rolling hills are few and far between. No undulating landscape, just flat, flat, flat MOUNTAIN flat. This sharpness rendered the skyline definitively foreign when I first came here.

The species of tree and bush that populate the slopes are different too. Much hardier, scrubbier, tougher, as witnessed by the high rates of allergy to native pine trees. The spruce must be so truly hardcore that thousands of years hasn't allowed evolution to produce a population immune to the irritants.

The waters along the south coast of Japan are far from inviting. Gunboat grey, cold and unwelcoming, in noticeable contrast to the warmer, softer waters in the Japan Sea four hours to the north. From Kōbe it's water that says, 'you'd be better off staying where you are'. I can understand Polynesian explorers setting off across South Pacific waters; warm, crystalline, inviting. I can equally understand an ancient Japanese population looking at the Pacific and thinking, 'We'd be better off staying where we are'. The Pacific is an industrial ocean, for shipping, fishing and - yes, still - whaling.

Kōbe lies between these sharp, bristly hills and the metallic ocean, an oasis in a harsh environment.

Two of Brunton's lighthouses are in the vicinity of Kōbe. The first once stood at Wadamisaki, to the western end of Kōbe Harbour, but it was decommissioned and replaced by a series of lights accessible only by boat. It was moved to Suma Seaside Park. The second, Esaki, is found on the other side of the Akashi Kaikyo suspension bridge on Awaji Island. It is still in use.

Kōbe is one of my favourite cities in Japan. It's cool and international in a country that tends away from cosmopolitanism. Other great world cities like London, New York, Sydney and Seoul

Wadamisaki Lighthouse

have a decidedly international feel to them; not just international brands, but cities with their faces turned out to the world, a plethora of languages rolling down the streets, cities that have outgrown the nation state and are almost as foreign to people from the rest of the country as they are to people from abroad. But Tōkyō doesn't. It's inward looking and reluctant to welcome guests. Many hotels don't have staff that can speak any language other than Japanese. The 2020 Olympics was going to change things, but Covid put an end to that. Tōkyō feels like it doesn't want to change.

Some of this is the legacy of history. Tōkyō, or Edo as it was known before the 1860s, is the capital, the seat of the Shōgun and his government. When the country opened up, it did so in stages and foreigners were deliberately kept as far as possible from the seat of power. Yokohama, 28 km from Tōkyō, was the closest foreigners could get without express permission. Kōbe was one of those ports opened, close but not too close to the Emperor's home in Kyōto (he moved to Tōkyō in 1868). Like Yokohama and Nagasaki, a strong foreign community grew up there. While it would be wrong to say the cities initially embraced their new residents, interaction between native and immigrant communities inevitably led to compromise, mutual understanding and a sharing of culture, the seedbeds of cosmopolitanism. The atmosphere survives today, physically in the preserved foreign settlement and the bustling Chinatown, but also in the relaxed, open, welcoming nature of the place. Not aggressively welcoming, like Osaka, but genuinely curious.

I've visited Kōbe many times. My first trip was years ago, a day there before going to Osaka to see Belle and Sebastian in concert. Minori shares my love for the city so we've made it a regular destination, dropping in at least a couple of times a year. For us it's a two-and-a-half-hour drive, highway all but door-to-door. A hotel on the waterfront or near Chinatown, depending on whether we're planning on a spot of luxury or gorging on dumplings. Around Motomachi Station there are a couple of jazz bars where we spend the late afternoon imbibing red wine, cheese and, ideally, some trumpet-based jazz. I have never been able to adequately pinpoint why, but there's something about the trumpet that hits me hard in the feels. In the arches under the train lines, we ransack second-hand record and book shops, often coming away with an original painting from the café that acts as a gallery and dealer for local artists. This is our Kōbe, these images of trumpets and paintings and rifling through vinyl. Perhaps trying to find an exact UK-to-Japan match doesn't work. Maybe characters cross cities. Rather than standing for all Glasgow, Osaka is the Southside: gritty Gorbals, gallus Govan. Kōbe then can be bohemian Byres Road, hippy Hillhead, classy Kelvingrove. Our kind of town.

We're aware that as we age, we dig these ruts for ourselves, get comfortable in our routines. Routines lead to boredom. Boredom leads to frustration. Frustration leads to arguments. Arguments lead to suffering. Routines are the path to the dark side. And Kōbe has such attractive routines. We developed them because they suit us. They suit our similarities, and they suit our differences. A trip to

Kōbe is guaranteed to keep us both happy. Yet we don't want to get too comfortable. That way suffering lies.

My first trip to a Brunton lighthouse coincided with an emerging realisation that I no longer enjoy travelling alone. When I was twenty, I got an Interrail Pass and wandered Europe by myself for three weeks until I broke an ankle in Lausanne and had to cut the trip short. I visited friends from uni who were studying abroad or had returned home after studying in Aberdeen, but in the main I was on my tod and I preferred it that way. I stayed in hostels and was forced by boredom to strike up conversations with other travellers, and when they got too much, I could just head off alone. It was the first time I'd done anything like that, and it got under my skin. Walking along the banks of the Seine in the pre-dawn haze listening to *Automatic for the People*, buying a baguette straight out the oven then catching the train to Lyon is still one of the strongest, most visceral memories I have. It's a morning that came to define my self-image, to stand for the kind of person I wanted to be.

In 2019, when I was thirty-nine, I went, alone, to Seattle and Portland on a grunge pilgrimage. It was a ten-day trip and six days in, I holed up in a hotel room, burnt out. That experience led to me finally admitting something: I was no longer the solitary person who walks moodily in the grey fog, hopping trains to wherever. That self-image needed to change. I still enjoyed my own company, and I still needed days without socialising, but when it came to travelling, I was much happier sharing it with someone. The problem is, there aren't that many people keen to drive for hours, look at a lighthouse, and drive back. So, the idea was to fold the lighthouses into more general trips, to, in effect, trick people into coming with me.

We buzz through Kōbe and almost out the other side. Suma Seaside Park is helpfully right next to the main road and we pull in as the winds rip across the water and through the trees, birling pine cones like excitable tumbleweed. The car park is empty but the beach is populated by local junior and high school sports clubs out for early training. A baseball team in their ridiculous trousers and matching crew cuts charge up and down the sand yelling encouragement to each other. A girls' volleyball team jogs by, urging the boys on to greater feats of showing off. The girls too have matching haircuts, a short, rounded style, somewhat tomboyish.

They must be a strong team. This haircut thing is common across Japan, an initiation, a hangover from more militaristic days, a way of fitting in, the extension of the uniform, there are many sociological theories advanced and as always with these things there's probably some truth in them all. The volleyball haircuts are taken as a sign of a serious team, a school and players for whom volleyball isn't just a club activity, but a calling. Volleyball is incredibly popular in Japan, particularly among women. It's said to be a legacy of the 1964 Tōkyō Olympics, in which the Japanese women's team won gold. The men got bronze. Japanese women's teams tend to be more successful than their male counterparts, something some (Minori in particular) put down to the different expectations loaded on either sex: men are expected to be strong and successful, and players often suffer under the weight of these expectations. The women - as women's sports tend to be around the world - are more of an afterthought to the authorities and are therefore freer. An attitude clearly and publicly expressed in 2012 when the Japanese men's football team (FIFA ranking at the time: twenty-three. Best performance in a World Cup: round of sixteen) flew to the London Olympics business class while the women's team (World Cup holders at the time) flew economy. Sorry, premium economy.

Along from the car park, separated from it by a copse of mighty spruce, a throng of children clamber over park equipment and play hide and seek. There are only two clear hiding places - behind a tree or lying flat on a bench - but it still takes the seeker an inordinate amount of time to reveal each hider. As we pass through Minori pulls herself up on the monkey bars, flexing her climber's muscles until she gets her legs hooked over the bars.

Rock climbing, or more technically bouldering, is Minori's prime interest. Towards the end of 2015 we decided to find a hobby we could enjoy together and to get into better shape. I'd done a bit of climbing when I was younger and a new gym had opened near us, so we went along to try it out. We both loved it straight off. There was one high wall for roped climbing but most of the gym was given over to bouldering where the walls are lower and crash mats deemed sufficient. Bouldering is both simpler and more difficult. The lack of ropes means you don't need a second person, and you don't need much prep: grab a handhold and lift off. It does mean however that if you fall, you actually fall. We stuck at it for a month, going two or three times a week. In October of that year, I was heading to Australia for my cousin's wedding. I'd never been down under and was really looking forward to it. A lot of my family were flying out from Scotland as well, making for a big reunion. The day before my flight we went climbing. I slipped, dropped, and went over my ankle landing on the mat. Reader, I broke it. Minori still goes three or four times a week. I went along once when my ankle was strong enough to consider it. Just the sight of another climber dropping onto the mats brought back the nausea and cold dread. Never again.

Wadamisaki Lighthouse today is a bright fire engine red. One of the first lighthouses planned (Kōbe was a major port at the time, while nearby Osaka was inconsequential), Wadamisaki Lighthouse was originally placed at the western edge of Kōbe Harbour (Brunton just refers to it as Kōbe Lighthouse) but modern technology and Kōbe's penchant for reclaimed land rendered it obsolete by 1938 and it was moved to this park in 1959. For a lighthouse, its placing is very much a denial of its purpose. There is no light cast and for most joggers, strollers and cyclists it is a colourful adornment to the front, a decoration breaking up the greens, browns and blues. Initially wooden, it was rebuilt in 1884 in steel. It stood 15.75 m tall and was illuminated on 14 June 1871. For most of its length it looks more like an oversized buoy than a lighthouse. Two hexagonal sections are separated by a much narrower central cylinder and capped with the usual crow's nest gallery. A number of plaques both on the lighthouse and alongside describe the illumination date and Brunton's involvement in the project.

It was originally staffed by three keepers. Three, as Emma Stonex explores in her excellent novel *The Lamplighters*, is the ideal number. The thinking is that if there are only two, and one dies, the other will naturally be suspected of his murder. The third is there as a witness. Of course, the history of lighthouse mysteries, such as the

Flannan Isles disappearance or the Little Ross murder, show the system isn't foolproof.

I take some snaps and pocket a pine cone that has fallen at the foot of the lighthouse and a small rock. These can sit alongside the sliver of brick from Shiriyazaki in what I've now decided is going to be a collection. The wind is blistering and Minori's interest in the lighthouse is minimal, so we saunter back to the car discussing lunch options.

'Chinatown?'

'We haven't seen the other lighthouse yet.'

'I know.'

'Come on, this is the whole point of coming to Kōbe.'

'For you. I want ebi-dango.'

'Hungry already? After. Remember, we need to do something new each time or we'll get bored and ruin Kōbe.'

'Sushi.'

'Okay, where?'

'Under the bridge. There's a roadside station.'

We swing out the car park and follow Google Maps through a tiny residential area which is, technically, the quickest route to the bridge, even if it isn't the best. Google Maps navigation may be the worst thing that has ever happened to quiet residential streets and sleepy villages. I've been taken by more surprised gardeners and inconvenienced kids playing in the road since turning to Google Maps for route advice than I'd ever have found on my own with a paper map. Soon there will be companies offering to remove entire streets from Google Map's routes for a fee. I, for one, would pay.

The Akashi-Kaikyō Bridge has the longest central section of any suspension bridge in the world, or so says Wikipedia. Other sources simply class it as the longest suspension bridge in the world. The bridge's English website calls it the longest bridge in the world. I'm going to give them the benefit of the doubt and assume this was a translation error. Akashi-Kaikyō is 3911 m long. The Danyang-Kunshan Grand Bridge in China is 165 km long. Not even slightly close.

It may lay claim to being the windiest though. The Inland Sea is something of a funnel and at over 60 m above the water it's a bit like being hit by an invisible buffalo stampede. It is frequently closed for motorbikes and yet offers a tour which includes climbing to the top of one of the pylons, some 300 m up. No chance. No way.

The Seto Inland Sea has probably been the most important stretch of water for the Japanese throughout history. Separating Honshū, Kyūshū and Shikoku, three of the four 'home islands', it was in effect the main transport route until the twentieth century. 450 km long, and getting as narrow as 15 km in places, it is speckled with 727 individual islands, making it treacherous for shipping. A lot of Brunton's work focused on this stretch of water, and it's a sea I'll be crisscrossing on this journey.

The classic book on the area is Donald Richie's *The Inland Sea*, published in 1971. Richie, an American who first came to Japan in 1947, travelled aimlessly around the Inland Sea keeping a journal which developed into a travel memoir. Richie died in 2013 leaving behind a legacy of scholarship on Japanese culture, particularly cinema. Amy Chavez has also written brilliantly about the Inland Sea in her book, *The Widow, The Priest and the Octopus Hunter*. It's an interesting, vibrant area, both near to the big centres of Japan - Osaka, Kōbe, Hiroshima - and cut off, isolated physically and psychologically by geography. Some of the islands are dying while others are thriving, embracing artists, alternative communities, and a rising trend for people burnt out by the rat race escaping from the metropolis.

We get all sushi-ed up and continue round the twisting coastal road to Esaki. There's little but a thin line of rocks separating the end of the tarmac from the ocean and the wind flings foam across the bonnet. Every few minutes I have to spray the windows to clear the salt off. None of this stops local drivers from hurling themselves round the corners at a disconcerting speed.

'There it is.'

I glance up from the road.

'Very funny.'

'What? Stop.'

I pull into the car park beside a 4 m replica of a lighthouse standing in the lee of a hill. Around it on the ground are compass points and images of constellations.

'Are you serious?'

'Is that not it?'

'You really haven't bought into this project, have you?'

'It's your thing. I'll come along, but you can't make me pay attention.'

She's half right though. At the far end of the car park, we find a set of rickety stone stairs. The sign at the bottom tells how they were seriously damaged in the 1995 earthquake and patched up. Coloured cement traces the frighteningly large cracks caused by the shifting fault line. The epicentre was a few kilometres south of Esaki. The Nojima Fault dropped more than a metre and moved a metre and a half to the right. The tremors lasted for twenty seconds. After more than a decade and innumerable shakes and rumbles, including the 2011 one, I still cannot even imagine what it would feel like to have the ground beneath your feet drop 1.2 m and move 1.5 m to the right. I hope I never can. Just climbing those uneven stairs, misjudging footfalls and tripping over steps, was enough of an insight for me.

The stairs trace the side of the hill and turn sharply left. Once they would have continued to the summit but beyond the lighthouse's plateau the trail is closed, the stairs evidently too broken to mend. Esaki stands on the cliff edge looking out towards the mainland, its role to light the way for shipping passing through the narrow strait between Awaji and Honshū.

Esaki is closed to the public, but there is a sign outside the grounds informing us that the water here, the Kannon Strait, is one of the most difficult routes to navigate in Japan. This was high up the government's list of sites for a lighthouse and one of the places Brunton would have seen on his initial survey at the end of 1868 as they sailed the Inland Sea. There seems to be some doubt as to exactly when it was illuminated. Wikipedia Japan helpfully gives two dates on the same page, 14 June 1871 and 27 April 1871, the Yokohama Archives give 1 March 1872, while one sign at Esaki says 22 January 1872. Whichever it is, Esaki is still fulfilling its function

147 years later.

Where the staircase turns there are two stone gate posts minus a gate. The chain replacement lies unfastened on the ground, so we ignore it. It's harder to ignore the low metal fence running across the approach and signs saying do not enter. While Minori keeps a lookout I step over the fence and circle the lighthouse, taking pictures, rubbing my hand against the whitewashed stone walls and collecting another souvenir, this time a piece of granite. A plaque embedded into the lighthouse above its entrance gives the illumination date as 1 March 1872, making me wonder how the more modern sign about 3 m away got it so wrong. Bored, Minori joins me for a selfie.

Esaki is a vastly different design from the classic tower lighthouse everyone pictures. Given its function, it doesn't need to be seen from afar, so height is less of a concern. Instead, it is something of a squat bulb with two square buildings on either side. From the ground, the light is only 10 m high, but has an elevation of 39 m. The whitewash is peeling, particularly on the dome, and the weathercock on the peak has seen better days. On the cliff side a newer, shinier light and camera stand fenced in. I hope the extra light is an addition, support rather than replacement.

Aware of Minori's boredom and the possibility of being discovered flagrantly ignoring a two-foot fence, we retreat to the car, nearly tumbling a couple of times on the listing steps. We continue down the coast, braking when white horses splash across the road and when locals crest corners on both sides of the road. Japan is proud of being rule-abiding, but when cars are involved, all bets are off.

We pull in at a spot where the Nojima Fault, cracked and exposed by the earthquake, is housed in a giant warehouse. There is something perverse about deliberately erecting a building on top of a violently active fault line. Why bother? To protect it from vandals? To keep it dry? The only purpose we can find is to stop us from seeing it: the fault line is closed. Please come back tomorrow.

'So, what do you want to do?'

'There's the whirlpool.'

'Yeah. It's after two. We could check in.'
'Motomachi? Art, wine and jazz?'
'Let's.'

5. *The Meiji Restoration*

In 1600 Tokugawa Ieyasu won the Battle of Sekigahara, establishing his predominance over the archipelago and ending the Sengoku Period, an era marked by incessant internecine warfare. By 1615 and the Siege of Osaka Castle any resistance had been mopped up. Ieyasu set up a dynasty that lasted for more than 250 years, ending in 1868. The Edo Period, as the Tokugawa reign is known since it was they who shifted the capital and centre of power from Kyōto to Edo (Tōkyō), saw more than two centuries of peace maintained by rigid inflexibility domestically and by keeping the rest of the world at arm's length via a policy known as Sakoku (locked country). It couldn't last.

On 8 July 1853 four US Navy 'Black Ships' under the command of Commodore Matthew C Perry sailed into Edo Bay and ended the seclusion and the peace of the Tokugawa regime. The Bakufu (the Tokugawa government led by the Shōgun) were given an ultimatum: trade or death, introducing the inherent immorality of capitalism to Japan on day one. Perry strutted up and down the bay, showing off US military might and generally scaring the government. Then he sailed off, promising to return in a year to find out which of his delightful choices they'd gone for.

His arrival caused panic in Edo. The two Opium Wars, where Britain used the same tactics to force China to accept a new trade treaty that allowed the British to sell opium to the Chinese market, were fresh in everyone's memory so they did not doubt that the US would follow through on its threat.

After 250 years of domestic peace, the bureaucracy had calcified and was incapable of making decisions. When Perry returned in February 1854, earlier than expected and now with ten ships of the line, the Bakufu had little choice but to let him land. Negotiations, such as they were, took place at Ryōsenji Temple and the Convention of Kanagawa was signed on 31 March 1854. Japan was no longer closed. Perry sailed off, stopping at Hakodate, another port opened by the treaty, presumably delighted with this bit of business.

He left behind him total chaos. The Tokugawa had ruled for generations through fear and now they'd revealed themselves to be weak. The fundamental premise upon which feudal rule was based - give me your loyalty and I'll protect you - had been exploded. Those whose loyalty had always been most conditional began plotting. At the opposite end of the country from Edo, the Satsuma and Chōshū clans (modern day Kagoshima and Yamaguchi respectively) were mobilising.

The rebellion started off under the banner of sonnō jōi: revere the Emperor, expel the barbarian. If the government didn't have the stomach for a fight with the Americans (and the British, Russians and French who followed hard behind with treaties of their own), then there were others who did. Ironically, they got a lot of help from one particular foreigner - Thomas Glover. By 1863 Glover was smuggling five members of the Chōshū clan out of the country and sending them to Britain to study at University College London. Glover was also running guns, ordering ships, doing everything, in other words, to support a revolution that would overthrow the Bakufu.

This volte-face from sonnō jōi to study abroad is both a testament to the complexities of Japanese domestic policies and to the open-mindedness of those involved. These were men of action, but also deep thinkers. This wasn't regime change without a plan. Long discussions, verbal and written, took place over what kind of country this modern Japan should be. The most salient example of this intellectual openness comes from Sakamoto Ryōma who, in 1862, set out to assassinate Katsu Kaishū, a man very much in favour of foreign trade. Before killing him, Sakamoto gave Katsu the opportunity to explain his thinking. Katsu did such a good job that a few days later, Sakamoto was guarding Katsu's door from potential assassins. To stand up to the foreigners, the thinking went, meant first learning from the foreigners.

In 1867 the last Shōgun, Tokugawa Yoshinobu, stepped down. After a brief war against Bakufu loyalists, the job was done. Feudalism was gone, the Meiji Emperor was in charge, Japan ratified its new constitution, and elected its first democratic(ish) government.

This wasn't the start. If anything, it was merely irrefutable evidence of a change that had been taking place during the previous fourteen years since the Convention of Kanagawa. Once Japan was open to trade, trade began in earnest. In 1858 the US-Japan Treaty of Amity and Commerce set the rules on how trade would be conducted. It was hugely unfair to the Japanese who, again, had little leverage in negotiations and little choice but to sign. This treaty became the precedent for all other treaties between 'Western' powers and Japan and guaranteed ill-feeling on both sides would fester for decades to come.

In 1865 Sir Harry Parkes arrived and quickly concluded a new convention which required Japan to provide the infrastructure necessary for trade including, importantly for our story, lighthouses, lightships, beacons and buoys to make shipping safer for all. To achieve these ends, and rather than slowly reinventing the wheel, Japan brought in O-yatoi-gaikokujin: experts from around the world. Richard Henry Brunton was one of these yatoi, setting foot in this political, industrial and intellectual caldera at the end of Meiji 1, the first year of a new, modern era for Japan.

6. Anorisaki and Sugashima Lighthouses

Spend long enough in Japan and you'll hear people refer to it as a small country. For example, my brother-in-law ascribes Japan's inability to progress beyond the round of sixteen in the football World Cup to being 'a small country with a small population'. At the time of writing Japan is ranked 20th in the world by FIFA. Number one is Brazil (209 million). Fourth is Belgium (11.4 million). Portugal (10.3 million) is ninth. Japan is the eleventh most populous country in the world (127 million) behind China, India, the US, Indonesia, Brazil, Pakistan, Nigeria, Bangladesh, Russia and Mexico. In that list there are five World Cup winners, all Brazil. Population size and effectiveness in a FIFA tournament don't even have correlation, let alone a causal connection. Size, it seems, isn't everything.

Yet the myth continues that Japan is a small country. I guess when you're geographically next to China and in the shadow of the US economically, historically under their thumb and still occupied by their armed forces, a certain inferiority complex may arise. This outlook leaves people baffled when they hear how small Scotland is.

My prefecture, Gifu, has a population of 2.07 million. Scotland's population is 5.5 million. The next prefecture over, Aichi, the one with Nagoya in it, where I work, is 7.26 million. There are more people in Aichi, one of Japan's forty-seven prefectures, than there are in my home country and my adopted prefecture *combined*. Size isn't everything.

Scotland is a small country. Yet we get everywhere. We often hide our involvement in the British Empire, like we were entirely absent, huddled in Scotland inventing *everything* while the rapacious English were tramping the globe with a colonisation programme on which the sun never set and human rights shoved where the sun don't shine. Yet everywhere you go: Scots. Have empire, will travel.

Scots still get everywhere, though in a less colonial, no-flag-no-country kind of way. It's a small world and sooner or later Scots, born or adopted, will bump into each other in far flung places. For instance:

Inuyama is a satellite town to the north of Nagoya. Once upon a time it was an important tactical centre, a crossing point on the Kiso river. Today it is mainly known because its castle is one of only five original castles classified as National Treasures (Himeji, Hikone, Matsumoto and Matsue complete the quintet). I know it because when I first came to Japan, I was posted to Inuyama. My company at the time, Nova, wouldn't let you pick your destination, but they did allow a vague expression of preferences. I put *'Not a big city like Tōkyō or Osaka'*. Country boy, me. Didn't want to live in *that* Tōkyō (9.27 million), *that* Osaka (2.7 million). Nova took me at my word and sent me to Inuyama (74,200). That'll teach me.

On my second night I wandered into a small Japanese bar. They were friendly and welcoming but the language thing was a problem so one patron took me to another bar. La Calavera, run by Kei. Kei is half-Japanese, half-Yugoslavian (Bosnian now, but he was born when Yugoslavia was a country and that's the word he still uses if you ask him where he was born). His family fled when the war started. He got out of Sarajevo on a bus that brought him to Scotland, where he lived and studied for a couple of years while sorting out his passport and refugee status. That bus was driven by a friend of my father's. Of course, I didn't know this when I walked into Kei's bar in June 2005. 74,200 people and one of them was driven from Sarajevo to Scotland by my father's friend.

Small world? I nearly fell off, to paraphrase Spike Milligan.

A handful of years later, when I'd moved from Inuyama to Komaki, a couple of stops down the line, Steve McQueen turned up in Inuyama.

Not *the* Steve McQueen, obviously. Not the one from *The Great Escape*. Not the other one either, the one who directed *Twelve Years a Slave*. Another Steve McQueen. A Stephen McQueen.

From Hamilton, Scotland.

We get bloody everywhere.

Stephen is my travel companion for the two Brunton lighthouses in Mie Prefecture. His path to Japan was a strange one, as most of ours are. Very few come on the direct route of study Japanese then move to Japan. Steve's ambitions lay in the police (jobs for boys of jobbing age).

'During the training we were doing unarmed combat Krav Maga. I was the attacker and was pushed aside. As I turned my foot got caught in the mat. I turned but my foot didn't. I was in a cast for six months and had to have an operation on the ankle. I was told I wouldn't have the movement I used to and that it would swell if I put too much strain on it.'

And that was that. No more police. Their loss, I feel, rather than his. Like the rest of us, he kind of washed up in Japan after that.

Mie is half of the jutty-out bit of Japan between Nagoya and Osaka, the Kii Peninsula, the triangle whose point sticks into the Pacific. The eastern half is Mie, the western half is Wakayama. There are three Brunton lighthouses in Wakayama but they are more than a day trip away. They require planning and logistics and somewhere to stay the night. The Mie ones are a couple of hours away needing nothing more than a text and a flask of coffee.

'Want to go see some lighthouses?'

'Sure.'

In an episode of *Blackadder Goes Forth* Edmund gives an example of the Germans' reputation for brutality: 'They have no word for fluffy'. It's not true, as it turns out, but I'm always reminded of it when I consider that the Japanese have no word for spontaneous. Not in the positive sense. All the Japanese equivalents are negative, implying chaos, unplanned actions that will end badly, disorganised, not proper. The closest is the borrowed phrase ノープラン. Literally, phonetically, 'no plan'. It's used on scoffing TV shows who interview foreigners arriving at Narita Airport with, shock, gasp, no plan for their travel. They don't have every night booked, they don't know where every meal will be taken, they haven't itemised every minute of every day. No plan? What is wrong with these people?

Spontaneous is a failure of organisation. A spontaneous pint is just not done. If I want to drink with my Japanese friends it needs to be planned weeks in advance.

Pint?

When?

The 4th of the month after next?

Can't. 25th?

Ok.

The idea of a spontaneous day trip is anathema. Not for Scots.

I'll pick you up in twenty minutes. You'll need a coat.

Stephen is about ten years younger than me and looks it. Blonde and blue eyed, his extremities covered in tattoos done by our mutual friend, Kei. There's a boyishness about him that makes people patronise him, dismiss him, but he's sharp and funny.

We race through - or rather over on the raised highways - Nagoya and follow the curve of the coastline west and south. I've been this way a couple of times before. Another friend, Debbie, and I went to Toba for the day to eat sushi and watch the pearl divers. The first time was with Minori. Our second or third date was to see the autumn leaves at Ise Shrine, the holiest place in Japan. Apparently, it's a bad place to go on a date, as the goddess Amaterasu becomes jealous and dooms relationships. So far, so good.

Steve and I pass the prefecture border.

'A new one for me.'

'First time in Mie?'

'Yep. Tick that one off.'

One of the curses of having people visit you in Japan is that everyone wants to see Tōkyō, Kyōto and Osaka. I've been to Kyōto fourteen or fifteen times, so a visitor who is keen to go somewhere different, somewhere you've never been either, is a huge bonus.

'Have you been to Kamikōchi?'

'No? Where's that.'

'Up in Gifu. It's a closed valley surrounded by alpine peaks. Utterly gorgeous. You can only get in on an official bus through a tunnel. Or walk over the mountains I suppose. Inside there's a huge lake, loads of hiking paths and families of monkeys.'

'I've never seen wild monkeys.'

'It's not much different from Hamilton.'

'Bit more civilised.'

'Lin Manuel-Miranda never wrote a musical about it.'

'True.'

About an hour out from Toba where we will catch the ferry to Sugashima and the first lighthouse, we hit roadworks. For some reason there is no ferry at lunchtime. 11 am then nothing until 2.30 pm.

'We're not going to make the ferry.'

'What do you want to do?'

'Let's head for the second one first. It's a bit further but we should be able to see it, have lunch and make it back to Toba for the 2.30 ferry.'

We reset the phone's satnav and sit behind a caravan of slow-moving cars, praying for a break in the traffic cones. Finally, after about fifteen minutes, it comes. Most of the cars drift back into the left lane, but the one in front of me stays right and maintains the 50 km/h he's been doing through the road works. I am not a patient driver with idiots like this. He isn't overtaking. He isn't going faster than anyone in the left lane. So what does he think he's doing on the right? Lanes are not difficult to master. If you can't master them, you should have your licence revoked. A gap opens and I undertake him, put the foot down and clear off. Prick. I have a friend who thinks undertaking is a shootable offence; he never seems to get that if you are driving correctly, it shouldn't be possible to undertake you. Undertaking is getting round an obstruction. If you don't like being undertaken, stop being an obstruction.

Almost immediately Google Maps pulls us off the highway.

'Fuck-sake.' The second lighthouse is beyond Toba but Google Maps wants me to come off the highway before Toba. At this speed I can't look and second guess it. The road curves left around a small tree covered hill.

'Monkey!'

'Fuck!'

A huge, blue-arsed macaque has stepped into the inside lane, trying to cross. I swerve into the outside lane to give him some room and we stare at each other as we pass. He turns his arse to us and disappears back into the tree cover.

'I've never seen that.'

'Me neither. All those beware the monkey signs and never a monkey.'

'Have you ever seen *The Last King of Scotland*?'

'No.'

'It's a film with James McAvoy. He goes to Uganda in the seventies, and he's taking the bus from the airport packed in with all these locals, chatting away. He sees a monkey out of the window and shouts, "Look, a monkey!" The woman next to him says, "Don't you have monkeys in Scotland?" and he says, "No. And if we did, we'd only deep-fry them."'

'True.'

'I saw that in the cinema in Komaki. I was the only one in the screen that laughed. Everyone else just nodded away like they'd learned something about Scottish cuisine. Deep fried monkeys.'

'I was watching this film the other day and they made a joke about obsolete technology, said something like, "You're the kind of person who'd still have a fax machine". In the Japanese subtitles they changed it to "VHS".'

'That must have hurt.'

Anorisaki Lighthouse is a bit tricky to get to. My distrust of Google Maps continues as it takes us down smaller and smaller side streets until we are driving on a single track alongside the sea wall. Dog walkers stare at us as we pass, and I begin questioning whether we're even on an official road at all. It twists and winds in a way that my 4 m long Toyota can only just handle. We meet a couple of small, sensible cars and have to reverse into driveways to let them by. Up a steep bit, round anther corner and the road disappears completely, nothing but a broken dirt track that curves into the trees. Google insists it's right. We have no choice but to follow. It opens up to a car park which, fortunately, has space to turn. I won't have to reverse back the way we came.

The wind is bitter. The curse of bagging lighthouses is that lighthouses are always - always - in the most exposed places. We walk through a well-kept park and along a tidy walled path that leads to a small wooden hut where they collect admission. It's only here that I realise that Anorisaki is open to the public. Like actually open. You can go inside, climb to the top. I feel like it's a surprise Christmas. I must look like a right geek to the young woman

Anorisaki Lighthouse

collecting the money, overexcited and babbling, but I don't care. After climbing the fence at Esaki and getting little closer than the wrong side of perimeter walls with Shiriyazaki, this is a big deal. I'll be inside a working Brunton lighthouse. I buy some souvenirs as well, a calendar, a key strap, a book about the lighthouse.

Anorisaki is a classic lighthouse, tall and white, high on a promontory, brass lights, portholes in the wall. Work began in late 1871 and a temporary light was lit on 1 September 1872, with the permanent light taking its place on 1 April 1873. This was common practice driven out of a desire to make the lanes safe as soon as possible, but also because Brunton was never quite finished tinkering with the lights. As I'll explore in a later chapter, both materials and fuel were subjects of constant study for him. 13 m tall, with a 33 m elevation. I'm learning enough kanji for technical terms by now to work out that the light flashes every fifteen seconds and illuminates the water out to 30.6 km with the brightness of what I think is 550,000 candles. I must be reading the Japanese wrong but no, luminosity is measured in candelas, the Latin for candle.

It was illuminated on 1 April 1873 but shifted back because of cliff erosion and then rebuilt on a solid concrete base in 1948. Photos from important points in its history and newspaper cuttings decorate the walls. The people who look after this one really care about it.

There are a handful of other visitors and we politely squeeze by each other on the narrow spiral stairs. This lighthouse wasn't designed for more than one or two but there's a happiness in everyone, a relaxed pleasure in the day out we're all sharing. Maybe it's a middle-class thing, or a middle-aged thing, but these kind of spots only seem to attract people for whom a day out is just that. A nice stroll. A pleasant day. A spot of lunch and a bracing wind. We take photos, wait patiently for others to take theirs, always smiling.

Sugashima Lighthouse

I collect another rock to add to my collection, have a quick look around the unenlightening museum and creep back through the narrow streets. We decide to get lunch on the way back. Google Maps has other ideas and insists on never letting us follow a major road for more than a mile. We get to Toba Ferry Terminal with about twenty minutes to spare and order a bowl of chips in the little café. At the end of the counter an incredibly drunk man shouts something midway between a welcome and a threat at us. Part of me thinks, 'oh a character for the story' but the idea of chatting with a man who at two in the afternoon is about to pass out face down on the bar top doesn't seem that attractive. What would Michael Palin have done?

I eat a chip.

Sugashima is in a miserable state. As an island it has been left to die. The buildings are decades old, their facades crumbling and filthy. There's a kindergarten and a primary school, though I wonder how many students attend. I have a soft spot for tiny schools. My first primary school had so few students they only needed two teachers, one for Primary 1-3 and another for 4-7. There's a tiny non-chain convenience store and a casual fish market. The streets are pre-car, too narrow to allow even one up, and scooters sit in ranks at the terminal, their owners presumably at work on the mainland. The walking trails are well kept though, and we follow the jags of the coast towards the lighthouse, a couple of kilometres away. Driftwood is stacked high, flotsam and jetsam. This is a working port with little care for aesthetics.

The path twists away from the shore and climbs. Sweat prickles and the coats are a hinderance now. Fruit trees shelter in mountainous folds. Side paths break off for the shore, little beaches, landing points. I think about writing a smuggling story set here. Rowing boats and communicating by lamps. Robert Louis Stevenson has a bit of a hold over my imagination. An abridged audiobook of *Treasure Island* when I was a kid, played again and again. I can still recall the tension when Jim confronts Israel Hands and the frustration as side A ended just before the pirates attack the stockade.

Mishima set *The Sound of Waves* on one of these islands, one of his best books. Islands are a storyteller's friend. Mysterious, small enough to encompass the imagination but pliable enough to support any twist in the plot.

Sugashima lighthouse is another squat affair, less than 10 m but we're high on the hump of the island, 54.5 m above sea level according to the sign. Work began in early 1872 and it was lit on 15 December that year, a fast turnaround. Most of the lighthouses so far have had at least some English signage but there's nothing here. Presumably they don't expect many foreign tourists to make it this far, hiking over the back of an obscure island in Ise Bay. The Japanese sign gives the usual facts and figures, a brief mention of Brunton, 17,000 candelas. The last paragraph loses me. I know enough Japanese to know when it's beyond my potential comprehension and this is safely in that zone. I point Google Translate at it.

I have saved many lives over the last 100 years. I pray that I will continue to cast this beautiful light on ships that go. It is something to do.

I read it out to Stephen, and we both laugh. That can't be right. I save it as yet another example to show my students as to why they can't trust machine translations.

The lighthouse keeper's cottage is missing and a sign informs us that it's been relocated.

'Where?'

'Meiji Mura.'

'Meiji Mura? Seriously?'

'Yeah.'

Meiji Mura is in Inuyama. Where we started our day. Dear Alanis, isn't it ironic, don't you think?

'I think I've seen it. I mean, I must have. I've been there a bunch of times.' Meiji Mura is an open-air museum of buildings. The Meiji era ran from 1868 to 1912 and marked a period of huge transformation in Japan. Architecturally it is defined by a blending of traditional Japanese and modern 'Western' designs. Meiji Mura was built to protect buildings from the period caught up in the Japanese obsession with knocking down and modernising. Frank Lloyd Wright's facade of the Tōkyō Imperial Hotel is there alongside saké distilleries from Kyūshū, tea houses from Tōhoku and, apparently, a lighthouse keeper's cottage from Sugashima. 'Have you been?'

'Never.'

'We should go. Take a few beers, it's a laugh.'

'Like the Little World pub crawl?'

'Yeah, but a bit more civilised.'

Little World is the other tourist attraction in Inuyama. A museum of the world, it has zones with recreations of African townships, Pacific Island villages, European villas, Native American encampments. Each zone is stocked with examples of cuisine from that area, and a few local beers. The Little World pub crawl is a drink from each represented country. There are enough that it's a bit of a challenge. Fortunately, the last zone is Turkey where you can buy kebabs. It's almost like it's been planned that way.

Sugashima is the last of the reasonable day trip lighthouses. There's one in Shizuoka that may be doable. Two of the ones in Wakayama are technically doable but it's a ten-hour round trip. I look at the map. Five done. Twenty-one to go. It's only going to get harder and more expensive from here on in.

A few years later, and Stephen is leaving Japan. After nine years, it's time to go. People either burn out or settle down. Stephen has burned out. Back to Scotland for a postgrad and a new career. A gang of us see him off with a Little World pub crawl, but a few weeks beforehand the two of us go to Meiji Mura and see the Sugashima keeper's cottage. We sit on the benches outside it, looking across the lake, reminiscing.

Friendships made amongst immigrants are stronger than friendships made at home. There's an awareness of pressure, of potential loneliness, but also of impending finality. Even those who stay in the country permanently don't always stay in the same area. I've said painful goodbyes countless times and even though technology makes it easy to stay in touch, it's never the same. No more spontaneous day trips with Steve McQueen, no more last-minute pints. The next pint will be planned months in advance.

7. *Yokohama Before Brunton*

The 1858 Treaty of Amity and Commerce between the US and Japan was the first of the 'Unequal Treaties' literally enforced on Japan by military threats. Some threats were carried out, such as when the British bombarded Kagoshima in 1863 in retaliation for the murder of Charles Richardson, a British merchant. Richardson is another internee in the Foreigner's Cemetery in Yokohama.

The treaty, which became the model for subsequent treaties with Japan by the British, Russians and French, stipulated the opening of ports at Shimoda and Hakodate (by the time the treaty was concluded, these were effectively open anyway), followed by Kanagawa (Yokohama) and Nagasaki, and then Niigata and Hyōgo (Kōbe) and eventually Osaka and Edo. The two aspects of the treaty that most riled the Japanese and contributed to the "unequal" label concerned duties and extraterritoriality.

Import and export duties were fixed at low levels that benefited the 'Western' powers and could only be altered by those powers. In other words, this wasn't free trade, this was extortion. Almost immediately Japan began pushing to renegotiate and it was to be a bone of contention for decades to come.

Extraterritoriality simply meant that foreigners in Japan lived outside the Japanese legal system. Should an American commit a crime, for example, he would be tried by his own consular court. From the 'Western' perspective, this was a common demand when dealing with governments that may not deliver impartial justice. From a Japanese perspective, it effectively hid foreigners from the law of the land. Considering Richardson's murder, it's easy to see the concerns of 'Western' powers: Richardson was killed on the orders of Shimazu Hisamitsu for showing insufficient respect as they passed on the road near Kawasaki. Under the code of Kirisute Gomen (also known as Uchisute or Bureiuchi), which had a strict set of rules, a samurai had the legal and moral authority to kill anyone of lower rank who insulted them. For a samurai, foreigners were very much beneath them. As the two parties passed on the road, Richardson was expected to dismount out of respect. He refused and was cut down. Two of his group, Marshall and Clark, were also wounded but rode off with the fourth, Borrodaile. Under Japanese law, Shimazu was within his rights but because of extraterritoriality he had no authority to carry out the sentence. The subsequent stalemate led to the bombardment of Kagoshima, and the very short-lived Anglo-Satsuma War.

Extraterritoriality still exists in some forms today, such as for US troops stationed in Japan. This leads to public outcry when they commit crimes, something that happens all too often. The *Asia-Pacific Journal* reported in 2018 that:

> According to USMC courts-martial records obtained from USMC Headquarters, between January 2015 and December 2017, 65 U.S. marines were imprisoned at courts-martial on Okinawa for sexual offences targeting adults, children and, in one case, an unknown number of animals.

In most cases, even though many of these crimes are against members of the local community, the offenders are tried under US military law. Needless to say, both the crimes and the fact that, from the point of view of the Okinawan people, the perpetrators escape prosecution in a Japanese court, are sources of tension between the two groups. The US military establishment is clearly aware of this and in the most infamous example, the rape and murder of a twelve-year-old Okinawan girl in 1995, the three men responsible were handed over to the Japanese legal system under extreme public and political pressure.

In 1858 the Bakufu had little choice but to accept the treaty and, once they had, were left sparse room in which to manoeuvre during subsequent negotiations. It was this capitulation, this sign of total weakness and surrender, that ultimately did for the Tokugawa dynasty and the Shōgunate. If you rule by terror, you rule by illusion. Once that illusion is shattered it cannot be rebuilt.

The next treaty was the Tariff Convention between Japan, France, Great Britain, the Netherlands and the US in 1866. Signed by Sir Harry Parkes, and representatives of each country, it was no better for Japan. It contains twelve articles, of which the tenth and eleventh are most pertinent to this story:

ARTICLE X.

All Japanese subjects may ship goods to or from any open Port in Japan, or to and from the Ports of any Foreign Power, either in vessels owned by Japanese or in the vessels of any nation having a Treaty with Japan. Furthermore on being provided with Passports through the proper Department of the Government, in the manner specified in the Proclamation of the Japanese Government dated the twenty third day of May 1866, all Japanese subjects may travel to any foreign country for purposes of study or trade. They may also accept employment in any capacity on board the vessels of any nation having a Treaty with Japan.

Japanese in the employ of foreigners may obtain Government passports to go abroad on application to the Governor of any open port.

ARTICLE XI.

The Government of Japan will provide all the Ports open to Foreign trade with such lights, buoys and beacons as may be necessary to render secure the navigation of the approaches to the said Ports.

Article X is interesting because it opens opportunities for Japanese entrepreneurs and students to foreign travel and trade. This is the kind of thing proponents of free trade talk about when they say capitalism brings freedom. A decade before, Glover had to smuggle the Chōshū Five out of the country and back in again. Now anyone with the correct papers could buy a ticket and head off over the horizon. While I am far from being a proponent of capitalism, this is one good that does come from trade agreements which is why it's ironic and depressing to see Brexit taking Britain in the other direction under the guise of free trade.

Article XI is where Brunton enters the story. Parkes contacted the Stevensons, and they in turn recommended Brunton. He arrived in Yokohama on 8 August 1868.

August is not a good time to be in Japan. Hot, humid, sticky and, given the infrastructure back then, undoubtedly smelly. Like Aberdeen, Yokohama was little more than a fishing village when international capitalism landed on its doorstep. It wasn't even mentioned in the treaty. Kanagawa was the original choice but in order to keep foreigners and angry samurai apart, it was thought more prudent to have them at some remove from the Tōkaidō, the main road between Edo (Tōkyō) and Kyōto.

The settlement grew somewhat haphazardly at first and the descriptions of Sir Ernest Satow give it a real wild west feel:

Streets were laid out with but little thought of the general convenience...Behind the settlement lay a newly filled-in tract of land known as the 'swamp,' still unoccupied except by the racecourse track, and in the rear of this again, across a foul marsh, were conspicuous the flimsy buildings of the Yoshiwara, euphemistically described...as an 'establishment for the education of young ladies,' and where a colonial bishop, to the intense amusement of the younger and more irreverent of the foreign community, had innocently left his visiting-card upon the elderly female who presided over the pleasure of the place.' [...]

The foreign community of Yokohama of that day was somewhat extravagantly described by an English diplomat as 'the scum of Europe.' No doubt there was a fair sprinkling of men who, suddenly relieved of the restraints which social opinion places upon their class at home, and exposed to the temptations of Eastern life, did not conduct themselves with the strict propriety of students at a theological college...there were also not a few who came there without much capital to make a livelihood, or if possible, something more, and hastened to the attainment of their object without being troubled with much scruple.

He notes that being labelled the scum of Europe so aggravated the 'English-Scotch-Irish' residents that all diplomats were banned from the Yokohama Club until 1865, when the much-respected Parkes brought about a new era.

Foreign residents were confined within a radius of 25 miles around Yokohama, which wasn't as bad as the Dutch had suffered on Dejima but still meant close proximity to each other with little chance of escape. While men of all sorts (Satow makes it clear there were few foreign women in Yokohama at first) came to this new frontier, it was predominantly a mercantile world with companies like Jardine, Matheson & Co (who Glover initially worked for) dominating the ballooning town. These descriptions can't help but make me wonder why on Earth Brunton chose to bring his new wife and sister-in-law with him.

With almost biblical inevitability, on 26 November 1866, a great fire swept through Yokohama, razing a quarter of the settlement and a third of the 'native town' according to Satow, one-fifth and two-thirds respectively according to Sabin. Lives, homes and livelihoods were lost, and those that survived were only spared by a shift in the wind. The fire led to calls for improvements and, given the prevalence of diplomats in the town, a new snappily-titled agreement, the 'Convention of Improvement of Settlement, Race Course, Cemetery &c. of Yokohama'.

When Brunton arrived less than two years later, the foreign settlement had been expanded to include the hills known as The Bluff to the east, but scarce other progress had been made. Brunton is haughtily dismissive of Japanese architecture and engineering, and is scathing of 'the primitive character of the average dwelling', the streets which 'presented the appearance of a body of water rich in islands' after rain, and the custom of collecting 'human excreta' in cesspools behind each house to use or sell as fertiliser:

Sir Harry Parkes lost no time in urging the local authorities to utilise my services in transforming the settlement from its unhealthy and disagreeable condition to one more suited to the requirements of western civilisation.

8. *Kashinozaki and Shionomisaki Lighthouses*

Like all the best ideas, this one is pretty stupid if looked at a certain way. Lighthouses are, by their very nature, remote. They stand at the edges, backs to the land. Perched on cliff tops, tiny islands or sharp reefs, their message is usually, 'Stay away from here' not 'Come in about'. Being accessible to the public is not a consideration. Brunton approached his sites from the sea and left the same way. Land was the problem; lights the solution. Lighthouse keepers didn't commute each evening, they lived in or beside. He can't have imagined that someday one of his countrymen would be trying to get here in a small yellow car.

The *Japan Times* sent me to Osaka to interview Brian Ashcraft, an American writer who was publishing a comprehensive book on Japanese whisky. I say sent. The article would run in the *Japan Times* but, print media being in the bind it is, the newspaper wouldn't pay expenses. The ticket and hotel (and I'd need a hotel. I was meeting an expert on whisky to talk about whisky and you're damn right we'd be drinking some of the subject matter) would come out of my fee making the whole thing financially pointless. In the face of a free copy of Brian's book and a night in Osaka drinking whisky with an expert, enjoyment before economics. If you get into writing for the money, you're daft. I got into it for the whisky.

Wakayama is not even slightly on the way to Osaka from Gifu. On the map of Japan, Wakayama is the southern and western half of the Kii Peninsula, the big isosceles triangle pointing into the Pacific. Osaka sits roughly at the north-western corner, Nagoya at the north-eastern. I'd already ticked off the eastern half with the two Mie lighthouses, and there were three more in Wakayama. Logistically, all three in one day was impossible - Tomogashima was a whole thing, with ferries, at the mercy of the weather, but the other two, Kashinozaki and Shionomisaki, are neighbours, both standing near Kushimoto, out on the tip. Without actually going in the opposite direction or getting wet, I am literally, mathematically, taking the longest way round. For Pythagoreans, I'm going from A to B via C. Still, it seemed as good a chance as any to bag me some lighthouses. I set the satnav and put my foot down.

I'd swapped the reliable but lengthy Toyota for a tiny yellow Suzuki Hustler. I was sad to say goodbye to the Toyota. We'd been all over Japan together, just the two of us hurtling down countless great wee roads, but I'd got a new job in Nagoya and driving into the city in a 4-metre-long gas-guzzler wasn't cost effective, good for the environment, or particularly feasible given the size of most city centre car parks. Woodstock, as I imaginatively named her, is cheap to run, better for the environment (though still not actually good, obviously) and can fit comfortably in most overhead lockers. I'd splashed out on the best sound system they offered and this would be my first chance to let Woodstock rip cross-country.

I left at 4 am on a rainy Saturday morning. Woodstock may have many benefits over the Toyota (which I now realise I never named) but barrelling full-tilt down a three-lane highway slick with torrential rain isn't one of them. Yet with Neil Young on the stereo, you can't not drive like that. I zipped past trucks, buffeted by winds and turbulence. Japanese highways are never quiet. Road freight is still the main way of moving things around the country and trucks are present 24/7. As I moved beyond Nagoya and entered Mie Prefecture with the rising sun, I hit traffic jam after traffic jam. Woodstock's satnav said it was six hours to my destination. Google Maps said four. I didn't care, I just wanted to get beyond Ise and onto the Kii-Hantō coastal road.

Since Shiriyazaki, that was the first time I'd been back out alone. Highways are all very convenient and when your aim is to put as much distance between yourself and the metropolis as possible, they do the job. Japan is full of great wee roads, and the #42 down the eastern side of the Kii-Hantō Peninsula is one of them. Hugging the coastline, separated from the beach by satisfyingly and worryingly low walls – satisfying because they do not obstruct the view, worrying because much of this coastline is protected by enormous tsunami-repelling walls and their absence along this stretch is notable. I've never been further down the peninsula than Ise. Woodstock's predicted six hours threatens to lengthen with every sudden swing into a lay-by to take a photo, breathe the sea air or buy local fruit from a roadside stall.

Lighthouses aside, there are a couple of less obscure reasons to visit Kii-Hantō. The Kumano Kodō is one of Japan's most famous hiking routes, a former pilgrimage trail into the mountains that includes an overnight stay at a hot spring. It's the birthplace of two of my favourite Japanese writers, Matsuo Bashō and Ariyoshi Sawako. The seventeenth-century haiku poet Bashō hails from Iga-Ueno, a small town in Mie that has many claims to fame: Bashō's birthplace, the centre of ninja culture and practice (the ninja house there is, hands down, the coolest tourist attraction I've ever visited), and it was one of the first municipalities in Japan to recognise same-sex marriage, something the national government still hasn't done.

Ariyoshi (1931-1984) came from Wakayama City. I picked up her novel *The River Ki* randomly in a second-hand bookshop in Kōbe years earlier. Before coming to Japan, I'd read little Japanese literature beyond the ubiquitous Murakamis. Japan had never been that bright on my radar and it's still something of a puzzle how I ended up spending the majority of my life here. When I came in 2005 I dived into the literature and history, reading whatever I could. I expected to be overwhelmed: embarking on a millennium of literary culture from scratch, where do you even begin? Luckily two negatives revealed themselves to be positives in disguise: the ridiculous price of new books in Japan and the paucity of literature translated into English (it's much better now, but back then there was little contemporary fiction being translated, just the classics: old dead men). I couldn't be picky. If it had been translated and was available at second-hand prices, I read it. *The River Ki* didn't look much at first, judging by its cover, but it's a wonderfully subtle story about the lives of three generations of women as Japan modernised. Ariyoshi spent her career writing about various forms of discrimination, giving voice to the oppressed and silenced. Sadly, there is little in Wakayama City to commemorate her.

This coast is also the home of Taiji, the town made infamous by the film *The Cove* for its annual dolphin massacre. When I see the sign indicating Taiji is a short hop to the left I briefly consider it but decide against. I imagine that apart from the bay, it's a pretty standard Japanese fishing town, none of which are renowned for their beauty or attraction for tourists. Besides, I bet they've had more than enough of outsiders. This is maybe unfair but I assume I'd get a cold welcome and as the sun is coming out, I don't want to spoil the mood by getting the brush-off from a local. I follow the road right and keep to the coast, singing along to Neil Young and periodically recording my thoughts and the sights into my Dictaphone.

Can I use your Dictaphone?

No, use your finger like everyone else.

I sometimes mistake the record button and when I listen back later to transcribe, I catch snippets of me singing 'Like a Hurricane' and 'Heart of Gold' ensuring these tapes will be destroyed for posterity.

On a map, Kushimoto looks like the tip of the peninsula but when you look closer there is a small island offset to the east, and the mainland hourglasses out again. I've tried to find a poetic way to describe it but I can't get beyond the fact that when you zoom in on Google Maps, the tag of mainland and the island together look like Kii-Hantō has a small pair of testicles, dangling into the ocean. Kii-Ōshima is the island and is connected by a bridge. Kashinozaki Lighthouse is on the eastern cliffs of Kii-Ōshima, while Shionomisaki stands on the southwestern edge of the mainland. The sea around here must be treacherous to require two lighthouses in such close proximity. I keep an eye out for Kashinozaki across the water but I keep getting distracted by signs for Kushimoto.

串本

Everywhere has strange place names that amuse visitors. Scotland has Twatt, Cock Bridge, Dull and Sandy Balls. Kushimoto isn't rude, but it is weird and funny. The second kanji (本) means root, origin. It's used in the name of the country: 日本. Japan. The land of the rising sun. Literally, the origin of the sun. So that's fair

enough, plenty of places use it. It's the first one that baffles me. 串.
Kushi. Kebab. It's one of only a few characters in the whole language
that actually looks like what it's supposed to. Two bits of meat on a
stick. Kushimoto. The origin of the kebab? I've heard some dodgy
claims to fame in my time – Kirriemuir professing to be the home of
AC/DC, for example – but is this small seaside town really claiming
to have invented the kebab? This is a mystery I have to solve, not
least because I'm now in the mood for some meat on a stick.

As I approach Kushimoto, I round one last sharp bend and
nearly crash. Jutting out from the ocean surface are a series of
seriously jaggy rocks, like Godzilla is pulling a Jaws impression.
It's stunning, with the sun glinting on the rippled water and
Kii-Ōshima in the background. To avoid actually ramming into any
of the other cars suddenly slowing down to enjoy the sight, I pull
into the car park of what turns out to be a visitor centre.

I feel quietly pleased with this turn of events. One secondary
benefit of visiting the lighthouses is a chance to find other sites of
interest I might not otherwise have come across. After nearly two
decades in Japan, I've done all the headline tourist things and pretty
much everything possible within day trip distance of home. When I
get the urge to travel, I can be at a loss where to go. Lighthouses are
in places I would never normally consider visiting and so this project
drags me all over Japan, into all those nooks and corners I'd usually
whizz by. I see the attraction of crazy bets and trips for the Dave
Gormans of the world: it's not the mission, it's what happens while
you're completing the mission. I'd hoped this would entice Minori
to join me on these jaunts but after Kōbe she's shown little interest
in my growing Brunton obsession, necessitating this solo trip.

I'd never even heard of Hashigui-iwa, as it turns out to be called,
and it's exactly my kind of place. I've always been interested in
geology, but from a distance, never really doing more than scratching
the surface of the subject. When I began planning *In the Shadow of
Piper Alpha*, for symbolism I made my main characters a volcanologist
and oil geologist respectively. I realised that I was going to need
slightly more than mild curiosity to back up these characterisations,
so I bought a bunch of popular science books (Richard Fortey being

the best) and drilled into the core of the matter. A little knowledge is a dangerous thing so it's probably for the best that I was alone with my enthusiasms in that car park.

I take some photos and scour the gift shop for anything non-tat. I love a good gift shop and I've yet to find one in Japan. Wherever you go, from castle to gallery to natural wonder to religious site, the gift shops contain the following: local food, usually pickled or sweet; local drinks alcoholic and non; crap for kids; and various cute characters only tangentially relevant such as the Kyōto Hello Kitty. No books. Nothing teaching you more about where you are. Just infantile tat. Here is no different. I buy an ice cream and sit wondering how on Earth the rocks were eroded in quite this way. It's like someone's buried a massive stegosaurus and left its dermal plates exposed.

Back on the road, the bridge across the water to Kii-Ōshima isn't your standard piece of civil engineering. The mainland ends a few metres above sea level, as you'd expect, but Kii-Ōshima is nothing but a cliff. In order to climb quickly up and onto the island proper they have erected the kind of spiral climbing road you get in multi-storey car parks only much, much bigger. It's a lovely piece of civil engineering, a moment of pure pragmatism: practical, well-designed and, utterly, utterly, ugly.

I quickly cross the island, no other traffic on the short and winding roads, nothing but wild vegetation, military chain-link fencing and some surprising signs. Beyond location and logistics, I've done very little research on the actual lighthouses before going, preferring to rely on museums and information boards around the site, so I'm somewhat bemused by directions to the Kushimoto Turkish Memorial and Museum. I'm on a spit of an island (Wakayama's balls) jutting into the Pacific on the opposite end of Asia. What the hell is the connection with Turkey?

I reach a large car park with the usual tourist accoutrements – vending machines, toilets, restaurant, random honour-system box of local fruit and veg – which seems overkill for the lighthouse, but no, it's the Turkish connection again. A beautifully paved walkway leads through manicured gardens to the memorial and museum which finally begins to offer some answers.

In 1890 the good ship *Ertuğrul* flying the flag of the Ottoman Empire foundered on the rocks off Ōshima and sank. The sixty-nine survivors were well looked after in these parts and taken home aboard Japanese ships. The dead were buried and the memorial built. All very neighbourly. The museum itself contains limited detail and none in English, only the bald facts in Japanese, so I get most of this off Wikipedia. There's a film apparently, snappily titled *Kainan 1890* (later titled *125 Years Memory*).

It appears this is the big draw in the area and the lighthouse merely an afterthought. Perhaps they feel it would look like sarcasm to mention the light, erected twenty years before the *Ertuğrul* ran into the same rocks it was warning them about.

Continuing through the park I pass statues, more memorials, souvenir shops advertising Turkish ice cream, decked out with rugs and lamps. There is a film crew with a reporter doing a piece to camera. Some of the crew watch me walk by and I worry they're going to grab me for the usual, 'Why are you in Japan?' talking head interview that gluts TV, but they just seem bored and are watching me rather than their colleague.

Kashinozaki Lighthouse

Kashinozaki Lighthouse finally comes into view at the end of the path, somewhat forlorn and forgotten. It's another short one, like a miniature Washington DC Capitol building. I'm getting the feeling Brunton prefers this style. Of the ones I've seen so far, only Shiriyazaki looks like how I'd imagined a lighthouse - a tall tower, strong and tapering, pushing the horizon as far back as possible. I guess, from an engineering perspective, this design is more stable, easier to build, cheaper. The classical towers are presumably saved for places where cliffs can't aid visualisation from a distance and where swell might engulf the light and all who sail in her. I can't help but feel some engineering knowledge would go a long way. I'm using common sense, experience and Bella Bathurst's book *The Lighthouse Stevensons* to reverse engineer Brunton's thinking. Mechanics are not my strong point as my father-in-law will testify, given I have to phone him every time I forget where the grease goes on my lawnmower.

Kashinozaki was one of the original eight named in the treaty. Work began early in 1869, alongside Mikomotoshima and Shionomisaki, the first three on the most notorious points. It was illuminated on 8 July 1870, technically making it the first permanent light on Brunton's watch. Mikomotoshima's temporary light was lit on 10 November 1869 but the permanent light had to wait until 1 January 1871. Shionomisaki was lit the same day as Kashinozaki, but only temporarily. It didn't get a permanent light until 15 September 1873. It is 15 m tall and shines to 440,000 candelas.

I'm pleased to see that this one is open to the public. Some effort has gone into giving convenient access: rather than going in at the bottom and climbing, a walkway and staircase has been built alongside it, presumably to deal with potential jams in the stairwell, wear and tear, and to keep us away from whatever you keep in a lighthouse now that everything is automated. No one else is here so I wander around the outside slowly, collect another rock and dodge the bees. They are everywhere, big black balls that hover at head height in the middle of the road. Some are harmless, some are unutterably vicious, and I have no intention of ever finding out which is which.

Alongside the lighthouse, the original keeper's cottage has been

Shionomisaki Lighthouse

turned into a museum. An expensive glass entranceway has been added, and an entrance fee. Inside the walls are stripped bare, the floorboards rough. An enthusiastic guide escorts me around, showing me cases of objects related to the house, like door knobs. He's really excited by the fact that some of them were made in the UK. Exotic! Others are made in Japan. Pride! He asks me where I am from then walks out of the room as I reply. In the hallway he asks me if I've ever been to the UK. I nod, ask him back. No, he answers as if shocked at the very idea. He takes me into another room and shows me the fireplace, asks me if I know what it is. I don't know the Japanese for fireplace, so go with 'the place where you have a fire'. No, he tells me. It's a danro. I shrug, take my leave with much thanks and check the dictionary on my phone. 暖炉. Danro. Fireplace.

Teachers come in all forms, I guess.

In the car park I buy a bag of local small oranges for 100 yen. What's the correct name for a small orange? Tangerines? Satsumas? I have no idea what the difference is, but the Satsuma were a clan based in Kagoshima, an area famous for its oranges, so the derivation of that name is clear. Like how China came to be the name of porcelain from China and then all porcelain. I munch them in the car enjoying the air con. It's heating up, the promised rain nowhere in sight. Satsuma. Tangerine. Mandarin. Who were the Tangerines? Does the word mandarin come from the language or from the bureaucrat? The world is a buzz of languages interacting, all these words that circle the planet being changed by transfer and misunderstanding. There is a preponderance of Portuguese and Dutch words in Japanese, and more Japanese words come into English all the time. Robot from Czech, schadenfreude from the German, shampoo from India. What did we use before shampoo? Real poo?

It's a ten-minute drive to Shionomisaki, back across the bridge and then through some wild forested roads. I pull into a huge car park. This time there are no signs for any attractions other than the lighthouse. This one looks much more like it's geared up for visitors. After a short walk through some lime trees (Tilia japonica, the species, not the fruit tree), I come to a small hut. They mean business here, and there's an entrance fee. I ask and the woman in the booth says it's a busy place, lots of people come every weekend to visit the lighthouse and walk around. Lots of painters, photographers. Lighthouses capture the imaginations of many creative communities. I buy some postcards and she tries to sell me a calendar. She looks so disappointed when I tell her I already have one that I nearly buy another. It's already April and she still has boxes of the things. Mine is hanging in my office, I tell her, in the university where everyone wonders why the hell I have it. I see them looking at it over my shoulder, puzzled, but they never ask.

Many people, I reckon, if they can't work something out for themselves just forget about it. Asking seems embarrassing. I've never understood that. I once saw a band from Sweden in Nagoya with some friends. None of us had ever heard of them but I knew the support band so we went along. Afterwards we were chatting and I asked how they were received in Sweden. One of my friends screamed my name. 'Iain, you can't ask that!' Why? What am I missing? Obviously, I've never heard of them in Japan, no one has, that's why they were playing to twenty people. It's not like I was saying, 'So I assume no one has ever heard of you in Sweden either'. When people who have never heard of me ask about my books, where they are published and how sales are, I don't think that's shocking. They are curious and whatever the answer (we sell out the biggest venues in Sweden, my books were all pulped after the publisher went tits up) are statements of fact, not opinion, and therefore how does embarrassment get anywhere near it? What am I missing? When did we decide that admitting you don't know something and attempting to find out is embarrassing? Did I miss a meeting?

It's a tall one, a tower. I never realised I have lighthouse preferences. Who knew? I like mine tall and slim, and this is my type. Kashinozaki is built in stone but Shionomisaki was made of wood. I can only assume it has something to do with height, flexibility in the wind and under seismic pressure, but wood is far from ideal and in 1891 it was rebuilt in stone. There's a lovely wall of fish painted by kids, and some watercolours of the lighthouse in a display frame. They have a contest every year for local schoolchildren to paint the lighthouse. I'm so glad the rain stayed off. This is beautiful. Not perfect clear blue skies and hot weather but that nice mix of warm enough and not a strong wind. Lots of guys off fishing on the rocks. A boat out to sea. I do miss living near the coast, the smell of the salt in the air, the positive ions. It's a bit like Okinawa, I think, a bit Okinawan. It reminds me of the cliffs where Japanese soldiers hid as the Americans approached, dug into caves, ready to die.

It's a different wind. It really is a different wind that comes off the sea. My kind of wind. I attempt to take a selfie with the lighthouse and wave the phone around trying to get us both in frame. I have never mastered the art of the selfie. Like trying to write in a mirror.

There's music playing inside the lighthouse and it turns out to be an actual museum, done properly. They've got a jigsaw puzzle. I'm sorely tempted. I could spend a lot of money visiting these places, buying all the tat. There's a portrait of Brunton himself, a big picture of the big man. There's a video, that's where the music is coming from. Somebody's put a drone up, filming on a nice day like today.

I've got to get myself a drone, they look like a lot of fun. It might be the only way I can see some of these lighthouses, the ones further out at sea, short of befriending a bored and generous helicopter pilot.

I go into the lighthouse itself, upstairs. Lovely wood panelling, I assume that's not original. From his writing and from what people have written about him, RHB doesn't strike me as a man who worried too much about interior decor. A practical engineer. Pages from each month of the calendar are all stretched out, laid along the curved wall. A gorgeous view out of the windows. This has obviously been quite heavily refurbished, the wood panelling, they've got separate stairs for up and down, which means they obviously get a fair few folk in. Luckily no one's here but me, so I can keep wittering into my Dictaphone, recording my impressions.

Oh, gods it's high. There's one more stage but it's closed. There's a cartoon picture of a man having his baseball cap blown off, which is fair enough, a good warning. If you're not playing baseball, you shouldn't be wearing a baseball cap. There's another couple downstairs. I walk around the gallery and I have to say I did not like that. It's really narrow and very, very high. The fact that it's on the cliff tops as well, I mean not right on them but close enough, why the hell did I decide to write a book about things that would mean I would have to go up high places? Geology. Back to geology next time. On the ground, amongst the rocks. Know your limits, Maloney. But there we go, that's two more in the bag.

Back along to the car. A bit of lunch then on to Osaka for whisky and work, the perfect combination. As I'm walking back the smell is as strong as anything. Tilia japonica. Japanese lime. From the family of trees that always remind me of the Nirvana line from 'Scentless Apprentice', a song about the novel *Perfume* by Patrick Süskind, the line in the song about how electrolytes smell like semen. Mitchell and Webb did a sketch about it, the smell of these trees. Queen Victoria (Webb) is being presented with a number of these trees to be planted all over London. She interrupts the ceremony to ask the shocked PM (Disraeli? Gladstone?) if he can smell cum. I assume these are the same trees. I've never actually looked it up but something here smells of semen and it's not me.

9. *Yokohama After Brunton*

Brunton doesn't dwell on descriptions and there is little of the poetic soul in evidence throughout his book. Instead, we must turn to Satow for a sense of what the Bruntons, Blundells and McVeans would have seen and felt as the *Aden* reached Yokohama.

Next morning early we were steaming over the blue waves east of Vries Island [Ōshima, off the Izu peninsula], passed the serrated wooded range of Nokogiri-yama on our right and the tiny inlet of Uraga to our left, and stood across the broad bay towards Yokohama. It was one of those brilliant days that are so characteristic of Japan, and as we made our way up the bay of Yedo [Edo/Tōkyō], I thought no scenery in the world could surpass it. Irregular-shaped hills, covered with dark-green trees, lined the whole southern coast, and above them rose into the air for 12,000 feet and more the magnificent cone of Fuji, with scarcely a patch of snow visible. The noble ranges of Oyama and others bounded the plain on its western side, while by way of contrast, a low-lying sandy coast trended rapidly away on our right, and speedily sank below the horizon in the direction of the capital.

Curious duck-shaped boats of pure unpainted wood, carrying a large four-square sail formed of narrow strips of canvas loosely tacked together, crowded the surface of the sparkling waters. Now and then we passed near enough to note the sunburnt, copper-coloured skins of the fishermen, naked, with the exception of a white cloth around the loins, and sometimes a blue rag tied across the nose, so that you could just see his eyes and chin. At last the white cliffs of Mississippi Bay [Negishi Bay] became closer and more distinct: we rounded Treaty Point and dropped anchor on the outer edge of the shipping.

Two years after Brunton left Japan, Isabella Bird landed in Yokohama on what is still one of the most bizarre, amazing and outrageous world tours of all time, one that really needs to be a biopic series. While describing the approach in the same glowing terms as Satow had twenty-seven years earlier, she is singularly unimpressed with Yokohama itself:

Almost as soon as I arrived I was obliged to go in search of Mr. Fraser's office in the settlement; I say *search*, for there are no names on the streets; where there are numbers they have no sequence, and I met no Europeans on foot to help me in my difficulty. Yokohama does not improve on further acquaintance. It has a dead-alive look. It has irregularity without picturesqueness, and the grey sky, grey sea, grey houses, and grey roofs, look harmoniously dull... I long to get away into real Japan.

In the writing of this book, before Covid threw up roadblocks, I travelled to Yokohama on the trail of Brunton. The lighthouses were why he came to Japan, but Yokohama was his home for nearly eight years and the focus of much of his work and intellectual energy. He opens his book with Yokohama and doesn't actually get to the lighthouses until chapter fourteen, although given the seemingly random way he jumps from topic to topic suggests he was writing more as thoughts came to him than with any narrative arc or specific structure in mind.

Brunton's footsteps remain to this day on Yokohama's surface. His bust, stone black and distinguished in the bright sunlight, looks out from Yokohama Park down Nihon-Ōdōri, the two most obvious legacies of his work here. Part of the convention Parkes concluded made provision for proper streets to be built in the settlement. Brunton drew up a report which was presented to Terashima Munenori, newly appointed as one of the Governors of Yokohama. Brunton was to report directly to Terashima regarding all the work he was to carry out in Japan, and he seems to have developed a strong respect for him, describing him as 'an able intermediary' who 'spoke English and had strong foreign sympathies' - high praise from the ever-dismissive Brunton.

The most pressing task was building a Lighthouse Establishment which included offices and homes for the Bruntons, the Blundells and McVean. This was right on the front – The Bund – at the north-western edge. Photographs of Brunton's house in the archives show it to be a large two-storey family home in an American style with a white picket fence and a large balcony supported by colonial columns. A model lighthouse was built on which Brunton could test prototypes. Today it is a car park with a small plaque. Eliza Brunton must have wondered what kind of accommodation awaited her in Yokohama and it's unclear where they spent the first few months until this home was finished, but the spacious interiors were all designed and furnished in the 'Western' style with some Japanese touches (screens and ornaments mainly, judging by the pictures).

Blundell was dispatched to Osaka almost immediately upon arrival, while Brunton turned his attention to local problems. He submitted a 'Scheme for the Drainage, and Improvement of the Roads of Yokohama' in March 1869. Before roads could be laid a considerable number of steps had to be taken. Firstly, drainage pipes had to be installed, which involved teaching Japanese artisans how to make pipes in the 'Western' style, since Brunton would countenance nothing else. After much trial and error, including laying an entire network that was crushed as soon as earth was piled on top, this job was done. Secondly, stone had to be found strong and plentiful enough to cover the miles of planned road. Nothing in the area was deemed up to scratch but a quarry was located in Shimoda. Having the necessary materials, they now had to manufacture the appropriate tools including a roller to flatten the rock and provide a surface suitable to macadamising. Once this was laboriously constructed, no horses could be found to pull it so he opted to 'employ human beasts of burden. For nearly a year a gang of twenty to thirty *ninsoku*, or labourers, dragged the stone roller up and down the streets of Yokohama'.

Nihon-Ōdōri was the greatest of these roads. The convention stipulated that a road would run from the port to Yokohama Park and thus separate the foreign and Japanese settlements. At 120 feet wide, it would also act as a firebreak. In autumn 1870 'the work was completed to the satisfaction of both foreigners and natives'. It ran from beside the Custom House - the epicentre of Yokohama - by the foreign consulates, directly bisecting the original settlement.

Yokohama Park, at the top of Nihon-Ōdōri (assuming you're

arriving in Yokohama by sea) sits on the site of the Gankiro 'entertainment district' which was destroyed by the 1866 fire. Brunton, quickly becoming the go-to man for jobs of this kind, designed the park in 1871 and, disappointingly for a Scot, included a cricket ground in the design. The Americans at the time also complained about the cricket ground. In 1929 it was finally replaced by a baseball stadium, imaginatively named Yokohama Stadium, so the Americans got their way in the end. The south-western side of the park marks the border of the settlement, beyond which lay a canal and the mainland proper - the 'swamp' as Satow termed it.

Much of nineteenth-century Yokohama disappeared in the 1923 earthquake but walking down Nihon-Ōdōri and along the port area there is still a ghost of the old town just slightly out of sight. In part it's the non-Japanese nature of the broad avenue, far more European than anything you'd find in Tōkyō or Osaka. Minori and I enjoy the stroll up and down, and through the park, taking photos, enjoying the nearby sea breeze, before she heads off to meet her sister, Chiharu, who lives in Yokohama. I head to the archives to dig through old newspapers and see what traces of Brunton I can find in the records.

The original settlement was isolated from the mainland by waterways bridged in three places, growing to six as the settlement spread east up The Bluff. Japanese bridges at this time were all wooden, necessitating regular replacement as the elements did their worst. Terashima, clearly as frustrated by the slow progress of change as Brunton, wanted Brunton to make something more permanent. Terashima, however, lacked both authority and funds for the project. Brunton, displaying the ambition and drive that marked his time in Japan and his complete disregard for his Japanese employers, 'recklessly' – his own word – decided to go ahead anyway in the hope that he could lead by example, quoting the maxim that 'nothing succeeds like success'.

Terashima seems to have supported this way of thinking: present the authorities with a fait accompli. Those who have lived long in Japan and dealt with business or governmental hierarchies will recognise the thinking: ask for forgiveness not permission. When I began working at a university in Nagoya, the Japanese assistant who effectively ran the department and was the traffic cop for every request, query and complaint told me, 'Don't ask me if it's okay to do something. If you ask, I'll probably have to say no. If you don't ask, I can't say no'.

Brunton got to work, asking favours of foreign blacksmiths, from people with the requisite machines, and scouring Japan and China for the necessary iron. His disdain for the Japanese worker was at play here, as he prepared the materials like a giant Lego set, presenting the pieces to the workers in a foolproof form where 'whole girders were thus fitted and riveted together by Japanese mechanics who...were completely ignorant of the exact character of the work'. He was, however, much amused by the idle men who gather round to watch the work in progress, smoking and passing comment on proceedings with the odd 'naruhodo' (oh, I get it), something I recognise well from my elderly neighbours who come to check on my work whenever I'm doing something in the garden. The bridge thus built was named Yoshidabashi and opened to traffic in November 1869. Brunton believed it was the first iron bridge in Japan but he was mistaken, Kurogane in Nagasaki being the first. The bridge was completely flat and was painted by many artists of the time, some of whose work survives to this day.

Settling the foreigners in this isolated pocket of Kanagawa kept them at a distance from the capital and the bulk of the Japanese population, but it also created logistical headaches for the government. Two of Brunton's tasks were aimed directly at bridging this physical gap between the representatives of the 'Treaty Powers' and the Emperor's court in Tōkyō.

The first was the construction of a telegraph line running the 22 miles from Yokohama to Tōkyō. This had been mooted a number of times before his arrival with both Swiss and Austrian representatives claiming sole rights to the contract without ever actually carrying out any work. The line was one of the first jobs Parkes tasked Brunton with and it set the tone for how Brunton would proceed in the future: ordering all the materials from abroad while training Japanese workers to build and maintain the system, developing a new instrument that could cope with both English and Japanese characters. The first message was sent in English on 7 January 1870, followed by a Japanese language message on the 26th of that month. Brunton notes with his usual wry amusement that the telegraph poles were 'slashed by fanatical Samurai who must find some use for their swords'.

Once the telegraph was up and running (followed by a second connecting Kyōto and Osaka), a trainline was called for. Brunton's preference was for building a system of roads that would later become 'feeders' for the railway. He quotes in support of this opinion 'a highly respected authority' who calls any people without 'proper facilities in travelling from a city to a town, or from a village to a hamlet' – decent roads, in other words – 'barbarian'. Amusingly, the editor of one edition of Brunton's memoir, Sir Hugh Cortazzi, former Ambassador from the United Kingdom to Japan, writes in his notes, 'The source of this quotation has not been traced. Perhaps Brunton was quoting one of his own comments'. I tend to agree with Cortazzi and would not put this beyond Brunton.

Self-plagiarism aside, Brunton is overruled and the railway goes ahead. Brunton's extensive experience with railways in Britain set him up well here. By March 1869, less than a year after arriving, he had drawn up plans for a line between Yokohama and Tōkyō to be followed by a line connecting Kōbe and Osaka. It took another year for the work to begin as the line was put out to tender, leading to several false starts as money came and went. The line was completed in September 1872 at a ceremony overseen by the Emperor.

I've read in places that Brunton also designed Yokohama Station but in fact it was Richard Bridgens (an Englishman, though Sabin calls him American). Bridgens also designed Shimbashi Station in Tōkyō, the other end of the line. Yokohama Station as it was in 1872 is now Sakuragichō Station, though the original building was destroyed in the 1923 earthquake.

By the close of his period in Japan Brunton was responsible for around forty buildings in Yokohama, in addition to the alterations mentioned above. Not all of his schemes came to fruition though, in particular his plans to bring safe, filtered drinking water to the settlement and lighting to the streets. The former was ultimately carried out by another British engineer in 1887 (despite a cholera outbreak in 1877), while the latter experienced a false dawn when kerosene lamps were installed but no one would take responsibility for buying fuel and maintaining the lights. Thus, they were 'postponed until gas was introduced, many years afterwards', though the first gas streetlamp was lit in Yokohama on 31 October 1872, implying that either Brunton wasn't aware of this development (unlikely) or, as he was not involved in it, was his usual dismissive self. His 'Scheme for a Water Supply to Yokohama' was published in *The Japan Weekly Mail* on 12 March 1870, while his paper on 'Lighting' - mainly for lighthouses but focusing on his preference for oil (Parafine and Kerosine [sic]), was published in the same newspaper on 20 September 1873. Both are reproduced as appendices in Brunton's book.

I spent most of the afternoon in the archives, reading Brunton's articles and epistles to *The Japan Weekly News*. Brunton, it turns out, was just as put out by his perceived stupidity of his fellow countrymen and other expats as by the Japanese. His war of words with another Scottish engineer in Japan, Henry Dyer, is also reproduced in the appendices of his book. In the Yokohama Archives of History, I also uncovered a book put together in English and Japanese to mark the 123rd anniversary of Brunton's arrival in Japan (the tenth anniversary of the archives, which makes more sense). The book is out of print and sold out, but I managed to track down a copy via a second-hand book dealer in Tōkyō. I also bought an A1 fold-out map of Yokohama in 1868 which I promptly left in Disk Union records. Its replacement now hangs in my office in Nagoya, confusing my students when they come to ask me a question.

Minori was more than happy hanging out with her sister, so I spent the rest of our trip in the archives plotting timelines, following tangents and failing to verify references (it appears some writers believe Richard Brunton, Henry Brunton, and Richard Henry Brunton to be three different Scottish engineers present in Yokohama in the early Meiji period). I did briefly emerge into the warm evening to visit the site of Yoshidabashi, today in its fifth, uninspiring

incarnation having been replaced in 1978, and to take a drink at the
Bruntons Craft Beer bar in Motomachi where the logo is Brunton's
top hat and the beer is delicious.

10. *Tomogashima Lighthouse*

The third and final Wakayama lighthouse is on an island called Tomogashima. It sits in the straits between Honshū and Shikoku, south a bit from Kansai Airport. Still uninterested in lighthouses, I talked Minori into the trip by making it part of a long weekend exploring the temples of Kii-Hantō with some nice restaurants thrown in. After work on Friday, we pile through to Nara, a couple of hours' drive, and wander the Friday night lights eating skewered chicken and drinking local saké. From there it's an early start to catch the first ferry from the terminal thirty minutes north of Wakayama City. There are only a handful of sailings each day, and they are at the mercy of the weather, so we're not messing around. I've learned from not getting to Kinkasan that a missed opportunity means having to go back and fix it later.

Tomogashima Lighthouse

It's just as well that we do - the waves are dramatic and predicted to get worse, so half the day's sailings are already cancelled. We'll have a couple of hours on the island before the last ferry leaves. Miss it and that's us for the night.

Minori is not happy. I'd forgotten in my excitement that she hates open water. She isn't a strong swimmer, the water giving her a reaction something akin to claustrophobia, and riding in boats makes her seasick. Hong Kong was a fun trip for her, with ferries twice, four, six times a day. She sits inside, a look of resigned loathing, and stares forward, willing the island closer. I go aft, riding the waves, taking moody black-and-white photos until a particularly large swell nearly sends my phone over the side. All of a sudden, the engines cut and we coast to a standstill. I listen to the announcement, half understanding the echoey, tinny PA. Something about a border?

Everyone is looking over the side so I follow suit. We're at a frontier in the sea, a clear break between dark and light, a current line. The water from the bay, water fed by rivers and circulated by the tides, is meeting the open ocean, the Pacific rolling into land. It creates this line and some massive waves, hence the caution we take passing over it. This, the Tannoy tells us, is why the afternoon sailings are cancelled. Once the bad weather comes this line will be impregnable to ships this size. Chancing it could lead to a capsizing.

Minori does not look happy.

Over the line, we sail down the length of the island and into the harbour. Tomogashima has a dilapidated, abandoned feel to it, like a once-popular resort on hard times. It's a different atmosphere from Sugashima, probably because it's so sparsely populated. Sugashima had an air of a large group huddled together against the elements, a community pushed together, like penguins grouped for warmth, their backs against the cold. Tomogashima is the solitary outpost kind of desolation, the community elsewhere, this place forgotten. It's spooky. You could easily film a horror movie here, or a series like Lost. A run-down café is tentatively open, but you can see the staff have no real expectations of custom. Everyone hoists their packs and walks on by. Driftwood, abandoned fishing nets, washed-up rubbish. Vehicles rusting into nothing, upturned boats, buildings hollow, slowly being reclaimed by nature, tendrils and roots searching for weaknesses. You could make war movies. *Tomb Raider*. I really, really don't want to miss that ferry. A night on this island would be terrifying.

Tomogashima, and all the islands and coastline in this area, are peppered with military ruins. Facing out into the Pacific, any one of these beaches could have been a landing ground for invasion forces. Gun emplacements, batteries, barracks, fading memories of a war becoming misunderstood and forgotten. Many have been cleared away, remembrance playing second fiddle to progress, but on Tomogashima they remain. There are five distinct battery sites on the island, as well as officers' barracks and a 'Navy Listening Station'. The first on the path is Fifth Battery, on the north-western corner of the island, there, presumably, for any ships that make it around to the far side. Cement and red brick - not a common building material in Japan, since even the slightest earthquake will render a brick wall useless, but strangely popular with the military. These buildings are hollow shells, each room devoid of any hint of use, occupancy. They are dark cells, humid and musty, overcome by encroaching jungle, probably full of snakes. There are ghosts too, echoes of the men who served here, who looked out over the ocean wondering when they'd see the Americans on the horizon, who watched B-29s pass overhead on their way to Osaka, firing tracers through the night. This is a melancholy place, a dangerous place. There's violence here; death.

In silence we walk on to the Second Battery ruins. I'd read online that this island and its ruins were the inspiration for Studio Ghibli's *Laputa: Castle in the Sky*. I tell Minori.

'No, it wasn't.'

'It was. Miyazaki based his drawings on this place.'

'No, he didn't. People just think it reminds them of Laputa.'

'So there's no connection?'

'No.'

'Oh. Well, it would still be a good place to make a film.'

Thanks internet.

A sign evicts another misconception: these aren't ruins, they are remains. The Navy deliberately destroyed them after the surrender so the Americans couldn't use them or learn anything from them. They blew the whole lot up. Much faster than letting nature do its thing. This also disappoints me a touch. I've always been fascinated, in a morbid, species self-hating way, I guess, by the idea of the world without us. Movies like *12 Monkeys* that show humanity being erased, novels like *The Day of the Triffids* that imagine us on the run, nature fighting back. Maybe it's an awareness of what we're doing to the planet, how it will eventually, inevitably, end up. There's only ever going to be one winner if we fight our own planet.

In the south-western corner of the island stands the lighthouse. It's another tall one, with a couple of attached buildings. It's strange seeing it here, surrounded by all the military debris. Such different symbols of humanity: one shows how we can use our ingenuity to make the world safer for all; the other what else our ingenuity can lead to. Our two faces, side by side. It pleases me that Brunton's lighthouse is still here, still beaming, while the Navy's buildings have been demolished. A spark of optimism.

Minori sits while I perform my usual ritual, walking round, taking photos and selfies, running my hands on the rough whitewashed rock, collecting a stone, trying all the doors just in case. Work began early in 1870 and it was illuminated on 1 August 1872. It stands 12.2 m tall, high on the cliffs looking out on the ocean, and made of stone. The sign says it was rebuilt in 1975 but in keeping with the original design.

This is number eight, nearly a third of the way there. I doubt very much I'll get all twenty-six. In fact, I know I won't. Wikipedia includes Tenpōzan in Osaka and Haneda near Tōkyō but I've been assured by locals that they no longer exist. At best there are twenty-four possible. Others, like Mikomotoshima, are way out at sea and without chartering a boat or a helicopter – two things I can in no way afford – I'm unlikely to get close to. Still, problems for another day.

We move on, explore more abandoned buildings. These are intact, unblown up, but out of bounds. Minori doesn't care, steps over the barrier, so I follow. These buildings were built down into the ground, invisible from the sea, even from the land. Steps leading down, down, into a silent, shadowy square around which empty black windows stare. I am pretty much freaked out. I've seen way too many movies to want to be here. Minori is the brave one. She wanders into rooms, comes out other ones. I wonder what was here. Is this the listening post? Barracks? Something more sinister? There are islands along the coast with rumours, some facts, about chemical weapons: experimentation, production, storage. Top secret, but locals knew. Ōkunoshima near Hiroshima – colloquially known as Rabbit Island – was one such island, known to have been a production site of mustard and tear gas.

At my urging, we leave.

The next battery is a network of underground tunnels, pitch dark rooms. We go through, phones as torches. Somewhere else a group of young men and women lark about, flirting, scaring each other. We hear their coy screams echoing as they scare each other. We weave our way through the tunnels, my skin permanently on edge. Spiders. Snakes. Ghosts. Tunnels have been a large part of warfare in Asia: I've been through underground command centres in Singapore, cave networks in Okinawa, I've looked down tunnels in Vietnam (you are not getting me down there, not in a billion years). War drives us underground, removes light, removes air.

Two young women suddenly burst out of a room. They scare the shit out of me. I scare the shit out of them. I get back into daylight and vow to keep it that way.

The Third Battery ruins have been turned into something of an art gallery. Installations in each of the rooms, despite no artificial lighting. We start looking around when I glance at the time.

'The ferry leaves in twenty minutes.'

'Shit.'

'Yeah.'

We're still only about sixty percent of the way round the island. We leg it, make it back in time, hot and exhausted. We grab an ice cream from the café and ride the boat home. The sea is disappointingly calm.

Because of the incoming weather, we're back in time for lunch. It's still early, we have most of the weekend and there's a gallery in

Wakayama with paintings by Saeki Yūzō, an artist we both love. I've got my lighthouse bagged, wine and art await. Following Brunton's lighthouses around the country has once again taken us in unusual directions and sent us to unconsidered places. Now's the time to enjoy these unintended consequences and keep Minori onside for more lighthouse jaunts to come.

11. *Brunton's First Survey Trip*

The Brunton party landed in Yokohama on 8 August 1868 and Parkes, delighted to finally have someone on the ground to deal with the backlog of engineering problems, put him straight to work. On 23 August Brunton dispatched Blundell to the newly-opened Osaka to survey the land for a settlement. His assistants were good, reliable men, but when it came to the lighthouses Brunton wanted to see things for himself and by November he felt sufficiently settled to survey the first tranche of sites.

Needless to say, they travelled by ship. Even if his purpose had not been coastal, travelling through the interior was all but impossible from a safety point of view. Rather than say this, Brunton can't resist making a dig at the infrastructure, writing that roads were non-existent. Here he is wrong. The Tōkaidō road may not have been tarmac, but it was long established and did the job. A few years later Isabella Bird travelled all the way to Hokkaidō and back, though she was one woman plus luggage, not a team of engineers. Bruton's dismissal of the road network – echoed again when contemplating rail networks – was based on prejudice, not experience.

Ever consistent, Brunton also refused to set foot on a Japanese vessel and demanded that Parkes requisition one from the Navy. This time his scorn was nothing to do with their engineering – at least not directly – as the steamers in question were bought from foreign sellers via corrupt middle men. Rather Brunton is disdainful of the Japanese ability to run these ships on a technical level.

His condescension isn't even logical: either they are ignorant or they are intelligent enough to foresee calamities. The superior tone – a father scolding a child – is depressingly familiar. He has no censure for the merchants who take 'worn-out craft, which in many instances had been laid up as useless' and 'speedily furbished up for sale in this new market'. An attitude I've seen all too often: if you're too stupid to know you are being cheated, that's your problem. He is clearly amused by the 'not over-scrupulous merchants' and agents who 'chuckled' at the doomed purchases. Being a conman is fine; being conned is a sin. Therein, the justification for both capitalism and empire. It was a subject Brunton would return to throughout the trip, devoting much more time to mocking his hosts than detailing his experiences.

On 21 November Brunton, Blundell, the interpreter Fujikura Kentatsu and a government official, Mizuno Tadakiyo, set off in the HMS *Manilla* (or HMS *Manila*, there is some dispute over the spelling across the sources but the logbook in the National Archives spells it as *Manilla*) under the command of Captain Johnston (again spelling disputes vary between Johnson and Johnston but the T is present on the cover of the *Manilla's* logbook in the captain's own hand). McVean remained behind to complete a full survey of Yokohama with a new temporary assistant, Samuel Parry. A depth survey of Yokohama Bay was also conducted under the auspices of Captain A R Brown. According to Brunton, eighteen to twenty Japanese 'attendants' also joined the survey, mixing with the 'blue jackets' (junior enlisted sailors) on the lower deck.

They seem to take a leisurely pace following the coastline, checking out bays and inlets, so it took them four or five days to reach Mikomotoshima, about 11 km due south of Shimoda, south-east of the Irōzaki point. Mikomotoshima was to be the site of Brunton's first lighthouse, and the most challenging. I'll go into more detail about it later, but Brunton notes that the island is 'a solitary rock, the summit of which was eighty feet above the sea, which all ships from the south bound for Yokohama had to pass'.

They spent several days sailing around the island surveying that site and attempting to land in rough seas. Late November seems a crazy time to be making a trip like this, which is testament both to Brunton's professionalism, his stubbornness, and Parkes's keenness to see work begun. The sea was so rough, in fact, that Mizuno proclaimed seasickness and demanded to be put ashore from where he would return to Tōkyō overland. Brunton is happy to see the back of him but claims that in fact the illness was a ruse thought up in advance so Mizuno couldn't (or wouldn't) be away from the capital for too long. Brunton naturally blames this 'practice of deception' on the Japanese character.

After checking out Ōshima (Ōshima literally means Big Island and is a common name around Japan. Brunton references a few of them without clarifying which one he means. This Ōshima was known by the foreigners as Vriers Island and lies in the path of any ships approaching Yokohama), which impressed Brunton, they surveyed points on the headland (presumably Irōzaki, where a lighthouse was later built) and received gifts of local sweet potatoes from the 'daimo' [sic]. Daimyo were the feudal lords of the area. He would have been a governor under the new regime but presumably language usage hungover into the new era. They also tried to buy a black ox but the local farmer wasn't keen on the proposed use for his cattle, so they got round this by 'raising the price offered, and partly, it must be said, by the practice of a little harmless deceit'. Deceit being harmless when practised by westerners for an end from which Brunton benefits; a tremendous evil when seemingly practised by Japanese against him.

Brunton, as I say, is light on detail about his trip but devotes numerous column inches to exactly what it is about his Japanese companions that most gets up his nose. At this point, it is mainly table manners that bothers him:

The curiosity they evinced at the sight of the table, with its cruets, knives and forks and dishes, was exceedingly ridiculous. Entirely without any knowledge of the purpose of these articles, they put them to all kinds of wrong uses. Catsup and vinegar were severally tasted and wry faces made at them, pepper castors were smelt with distressing results, and beef or mutton looked at askance. For the first few meals the Europeans were kept in uncontrollable fits of laughter... Nevertheless, as illustrating their extraordinary adaptability to violent change, two or three days only had elapsed before these Japanese seemed to comport themselves at meals as well-bred Europeans would.

Were I Mizuno, I too would want to get as far as possible from these rude Europeans who think that not knowing the appropriate use of a cruet-stand (me neither) is ridiculous but openly laughing at your guests, including a representative of the Emperor present on board a Navy vessel, is seemingly not a breach of manners or diplomatic decorum. It must have taken every diplomatic bone in Mizuno's body to fake seasickness rather than tell Brunton to 'take your catsup and fuck right off, big nose'.

They continued on their leisurely journey stopping at various other sites along the way. Between Irōzaki and Kōbe are the locations of Omaezaki, Anorisaki, Sugashima, Kashinozaki, Shionomisaki, and Tomogashima lighthouses, plus Esaki on Awaji Island, Wadamisaki in Kōbe, and Tenpōzan at Osaka. The government had already ordered lights for Mikomotoshima, (Shizuoka), Iojima (Nagasaki), Satamisaki (Kagoshima), Hakodate and Yokohama harbours, Kashinozaki, Shionomisaki, and Tomogashima (all in Wakayama), Esaki (Hyōgo), Hesaki (Fukuoka), Mutsurejima (called Rokurenjima by Brunton, an alternative reading of the kanji, in Yamaguchi), Wadamisaki (Kōbe) and Tenpōzan (Osaka).

From Kōbe he rides to Osaka where he makes a survey of the river. Osaka had been officially opened to foreign trade on 1 September 1868, but a sand bar across Yodogawa (Yodo River) meant none but the shallowest of drafts could pass and so thus 'nullified the long and wearisome negotiations [Osaka was due to be opened on 1 January 1863 and delayed more than five years] and infinite labour from which its opening resulted'.

Brunton met Governor Godai, 'a man of advanced ideas' which, we slowly learn, is a Brunton euphemism for 'Japanese who listens to me', who explained the current plan. Brunton dismisses it out of hand and prepares his own report during the few days they remain in Osaka. He names Parkes as being in favour of the plan, but the bureaucracy in Tōkyō baulked at the cost. Brunton later reports that Parkes learned the work had gone ahead under the auspices of the River Departments, a branch of the government over which Godai had no control and the work was being done without – shock horror – foreign supervision. Brunton immediately dispatches Blundell who, of course, reports back that they're doing it all wrong. Blundell must have been as diplomatic as his boss because he was chased from the site and pelted with stones. Godai, upon receiving Blundell's report, stops the work. Brunton notes with obvious satisfaction that they wasted about $250,000 and that Osaka remained effectively closed, with goods being sent to Kōbe by the new railroad and shipped from there. A victory for none, though Brunton is clearly claiming the points.

During the layover in Kansai, Brunton also meets Itō Shunsuke (also known as Hirobumi, one of the Chōshū Five smuggled out of Japan by Glover and sent to Britain. When Brunton met him, he was Governor of Hyōgo and would become Japan's first prime minister in 1885) who requested that Brunton build a telegraph linking Kōbe and Osaka. It's interesting to note that while the Japanese records show he met Itō, Brunton doesn't mention it and in fact writes that he first met Itō on 20 December 1869.

What he does mention, in great sardonic detail, is meeting another 'official of high rank', Ueno Kagenori, who had come from Kyōto with the express intention of overseeing the rest of the trip. This official, Brunton says, refused to travel on the British ship and requested (Brunton's word, though 'ordered' or 'demanded' is more fitting with the impression Brunton paints) that everyone leave the *Manilla* and sail on his ship. Brunton, of course, refused, remaining intransigent in the face of a potential diplomatic incident. In fact, Brunton takes great delight in telling the dignitary the provenance of the ship he has bought:

Well known to mariners who were in the habit of visiting Shanghai, she had been employed for very many years as a tug-boat on the Chinese rivers. When worn out, she had been laid up on the bank as having seen her best days…I lost no time in informing my Japanese friend of the character of his purchase, and was not surprised to learn soon after that he had abandoned her.

The stalemate continued, however, with Ueno chartering the *Argus* from a British merchant and the two boats continuing through the Inland Sea, stopping off on the way.

The Inland Sea was essentially unnavigable at night. Brunton's aim wasn't to allow twenty-four-hour shipping, but more realistically to make 'a considerable portion of the sea…navigable by night, and vessels would be guided to places where they might anchor with safety and wait for daylight'.

Using Hiroshima Island (not the same place as the city, just the same name, unhelpfully) as a base to draw fresh water and supplies, they surveyed the cluttered but beautiful waters of the Seto Inland Sea deciding where to best position the lighthouses, lightships and beacons. He had three criteria:

1. To avoid redundancy, leaving no light where land could be clearly seen, even at night, or where there were no hidden dangers.

2. Where channels became dangerous during 'dark weather'.

3. Where a light would turn a route from difficult to easy, or where it was easy to get confused between similar-looking islands.

Tragedy struck the *Manilla* when Frank Toovey Lake, a nineteen-year-old navigating midshipman, died. The exact cause of death is not recorded but Graham Thomas in his book on Lake suggests that cholera or some other form of dysentery was likely picked up during their sojourn in Osaka. Fresh water was still an issue at this time, as Brunton's urgency regarding drainage and the building of a water system in Yokohama illustrates. There would be numerous cholera outbreaks over the next few years until the situation was remedied. Thomas also speculates that Lake and Brunton would have come into close contact, given the size of the *Manilla*, and that Lake may even have helped in his surveys, since Lake's father was also a civil engineer. No evidence for this remains, however, and Brunton never refers to Lake by name. He does attend the funeral on Hiroshima Island. Brunton is moved by the respectful nature of the ceremony and burial and says that his opinion of Japan was greatly enhanced by this experience. He even returned a few years later to pay his respects. Lake's grave stands on Hiroshima to this day, and after speaking with Thomas, I decided I too needed to make this trip (see chapter 28).

Lake was buried on the morning of 21 December, and afterwards they set sail, continuing to Shimonoseki (where the sea narrows into the straits that separate Honshū and Kyūshū), landing at Himeshima on the 22nd. Along the way they lost the *Argus*. Paying a visit to the governor at Shimonoseki, they waited in vain for Ueno to show up. Eventually, on 23 December, they left for Nagasaki, surveying

Hesaki (not to be confused with Esaki) and Mutsurejima, arriving on Christmas Eve. The *Argus* showed up the next day, something of a Christmas present for Brunton, since the passengers weren't aboard. He revels in the news that it had run aground near Shimonoseki and had to be refloated. However, fearing more bad luck, the party had decided to travel overland.

Nagasaki appealed to Brunton, as it does to many, describing the harbour as 'one of the most beautiful, even as it is the safest in the world'. Nagasaki had been the single porous point in Japan's enclosure for hundreds of years and so when the treaties opened the port fully beyond the tiny island of Dejima, it had a head start on Yokohama. Brunton met the governor, Inoue, who was fluent in English after an education in the US, so Brunton wasted no time in telling him all about Ueno's escapades. He doesn't mention meeting Glover, though as they were in Nagasaki at the same time, the two Scots must have crossed paths. He does mention that Glover was involved in opening the island of Takashima for its coal and visited the mine. After a few days Ueno and his retinue showed up, presumably to much mocking from Brunton. Rather than set foot on the *Manilla* however, Ueno decides to cut his losses and heads home overland. Brunton was happy to see the back of him but was worried that Ueno's expenses (two ships and a large retinue for 'not one atom of useful work' achieved through 'ignorant bumptiousness, dignified stupidity, and unreasonable stubbornness') would be taken from the lighthouse budget.

After surveying the island of Iojima (not that one), the *Manilla* sailed to Satamisaki, the southernmost point of the Japanese 'home' islands, formerly Satsuma, now Kagoshima. With high seas and no safe anchorage, a survey was abandoned for a later date, and the ship set course for home, stopping off at Hiroshima to check on Lake's grave and take on water, returning to Yokohama on 5 January 1869.

Overall, it seems this was a successful trip. Work on this first round of lighthouses began once the weather cleared up in later spring and summer, while McVean's survey of Yokohama conducted in the meantime produced a highly-accurate plan of the settlement and the basis for all the subsequent improvements made under

Brunton's supervision.

Brunton would make further trips, including one back to Satamisaki, around to Niigata on the Japan Sea coast, and later to Okinawa, but it's this initial survey that provided his education in both the landscape he was dealing with and the sort of help or hinderance he could expect from local rulers and workers. By the end of 1868 Brunton's opinions about Japan had been formed and set, and he was ready to go to work.

12. *The Support Team*

FUJIKURA KENTATSU

I have no idea how good Brunton's Japanese was by 1876 but I'd imagine he had all the nouns he needed to do his business and all the adjectives required to insult whoever deserved it that day. Most of his superiors and the officials assigned to his work could speak English. For some time after Perry's arrival Dutch was the lingua-franca of Japan, since it was really the only European language anyone in Japan had been exposed to, but with America being the big threat, much energy was devoted to studying their language. Like most English-speaking immigrants to Japan (myself included for longer than I'd care to admit) he probably had enough Japanese to get by and relied on help for the rest.

Brunton rarely makes mention of the language except to massacre it with phonetic spellings. He does however briefly namecheck his interpreter, Fujikura Kentatsu, offering one of the few unreserved moments of praise for a Japanese person in the book.

Fujikura was the son of a doctor, born in 1851 in the Zeze Domain, what is now part of Shiga Prefecture (east of Kyōto). One of the first generation born into a Japanese world with 'Westerners' in it, he saw the opportunities there and went to Yokohama in 1865 at the age of fourteen or fifteen to study English. This seems to have been a common path on both sides - go as a student, learn the language, become an interpreter which allows you access to important rooms filled with powerful people, use your connections to move into other areas. Satow built his entire career this way, as did Fujikura. He was hired as interpreter from Brunton's arrival in 1868, travelled with him on the 1868 survey, and was involved in all aspects of Brunton's work and personal life day-to-day. In doing so he had the best education in civil engineering imaginable and it's easy to see Brunton taking a shine to this bright, curious teenager. In April 1872 Brunton helped arrange for Fujikura to study engineering for two years at the University of Edinburgh, under the supervision of the Stevensons.

Upon Fujikura's return to Japan in July 1874 Brunton hired him as his assistant, and when Brunton left in 1876 he took over as chief. Fujikura was responsible for the first concrete lighthouse in Japan, Kurasaki in Miyazaki Prefecture in 1884. He continued to climb up the bureaucracy, rising through the Ministry of Industry and then the Ministry of Communications. He died at the age of 83 in 1934.

The photo of Fujikura in the Yokohama Archives' book on Brunton shows him in his later years: a long, thin face with barely an ounce of fat on him. Strong jaw adorned with a grey beard, close-cropped grey hair and dark, prominent eyebrows. He is looking down slightly, off camera, thoughtful, perhaps a touch melancholy, but there's humour in his eyes. This is a man who has travelled, who has experienced a lot in a rollercoaster century, part of the first generation to bridge the divide between Japan and the outside, between the feudal past and the modern future. He lived through the promise and the corruption of that promise and died before the endgame of modernisation played out in the Pacific theatre. In the portrait is a man with stories to tell.

TERASHIMA MUNENORI

In October 1868 Terashima Munenori became a governor of Yokohama and was appointed as Brunton's direct superior. Brunton describes him as a man 'who spoke English and had strong foreign sympathies…he was an able intermediary between the Imperial Government and the representatives of the Treaty Powers'.

Brunton got most of his instructions from Terashima and had to run everything by him. The two seemed to get on well and Brunton portrays Terashima as being on his side against the frustrations of the system. It was Terashima, for example, who urged Brunton to go ahead with the iron bridge at Yoshida 'as he desired to show his countrymen how bridges were built in Western countries'.

Born in Satsuma (Kagoshima) in 1832, Terashima was deeply involved in the politics of the age and is described by William Elliot

Griffis in his introduction to Brunton's book as one of the 'ablest of the Mikado's statesmen in these early years'. He spoke Dutch and English, spent 1865-7 in Britain, and would be sent as Japan's first ambassador to Britain from 1872-3 and in 1883 as ambassador to the US.

As I read about Terashima in the Japanese sources, I got the usual feeling of vertigo trying to work out his timeline, his career trajectory and his duties, making something of a spider diagram than a straight chronology, so it was with deep relief that I read the following translation from his autobiography in the Yokohama Archives' book on Brunton:

> I was only in Yokohama for one and a half years, but since the duties of government officials were not yet clearly defined in those days, I not only performed the current duties of the governor of Kanagawa, but served as Councillor for Foreign Affairs, judge, and head of the Yokosuka Arsenal, as well as oversaw the construction of lighthouses and a telegraph system.

He had all of these jobs and responsibilities at the same time because there was no system, no real civil service. There had just been a revolution and these men were inventing the new system as they went along. In a sense it was a real time for meritocracy, and you can see it at work in the career of someone like Terashima - we need an able man, Terashima is an able man, therefore give him the job. Brunton certainly thought so. Given some of Terashima's successors, it doesn't seem too big a leap to speculate that for all the headaches Brunton endured, without someone like Terashima in charge he would have been a lot less successful.

That's not to say that Terashima was working against his own government; he was just far more pragmatic than many of his colleagues. Brunton shows the heart of Terashima's motivation when the issue of coal mining in Japan is raised. He paraphrases Terashima as saying:

The minerals of Japan belonged to the Japanese, that there was no fear of their deteriorating through keeping, and that they must remain unoperated on until the Japanese themselves were in a position to work them.

He embraced what the 'West' had to teach but was never in any doubt that this was a process that would end, as we saw with Fujikura's career, with the Japanese fully in control of their nation and its destiny.

Terashima died in 1893 aged sixty.

COLIN ALEXANDER MCVEAN

Born on Iona in 1838 where his father was the minister, McVean studied in Edinburgh, returning to the Hebrides as part of the Hydrographic Office where he conducted surveys. He travelled to Turkey and Bulgaria building railways and married Mary Wood Cowan from Penicuik shortly before travelling to Japan.

As Assistant Engineer along with Blundell, he was to be paid $150 a month, a sum which he quickly discovered was insufficient on which to live in Yokohama. Brunton was sympathetic and intervened on their behalf, writing to Parkes:

A man arriving in a country like this has many causes for discontent. The nature of his duties disappoints him. He is required, owing to his being the only engineer, to do trifling pieces of work which perhaps before had been given over to his juniors in the office. He is often required then to explain the minutest details to men unwilling to execute them. He has to deal with people tantalisingly slow and lazy and who are wonderfully retentive of their own system of working. All European articles of food and clothing are three times the price they are at home...therefore a man who exchanges say, £300 a year at home for £800 a year here with the prospect of bettering himself is grievously disappointed. These things should be explained directly to anyone coming here and he should not be allowed to come out in ignorance of them.

They were offered a raise to $300 (Brunton was on $450, rising to $600 in 1870) but that was still too low a salary for the high cost of living.

McVean was put in day-to-day charge of Mikomotoshima, moving to Shimoda from March to June 1869 to oversee the work, bringing his new-born daughter along. He wasn't happy with the output of the local masons and asked Brunton for permission to change the design to fit in with what was possible. Dissatisfied with Brunton's reply and smarting over the money, McVean resigned at the start of September 1869 and set up his own company, Vulcan Foundry. In December 1869 he was officially replaced by Samuel Parry, who had been hired as McVean's assistant the previous December.

McVean went on to become chief surveyor for the government's newly-established Survey Department and was involved in surveying and mapping the whole country. He was also called on to help build the new engineering college and engaged in rebuilding Tōkyō after the 1872 fire (as was Brunton). McVean took the official readings in Japan of the transit of Venus in 1874.

His employment in Japan ended in 1876 (as did Brunton's) and he returned to Scotland via the US taking a vast collection of Japanese art with him. In Edinburgh, the McVeans became friends with Isabella Bird and it was their advice and network of contacts that were instrumental in her visit to Japan in 1878. McVean retired to Mull in 1885.

As always, there is nothing written about personal relationships and day-to-day interactions at this time but given the size of the foreign settlement and the even smaller circle of civil engineers in Yokohama, Brunton and McVean must have been in regular contact. Did Brunton see McVean as a competitor? As a traitor? Or since there was more than enough work to go around did his professionalism rejoice that another good British engineer was ensuring things were done properly? My instinct leans towards the latter. Brunton wasn't one to pull his punches and was quite happy to make public his frustration with and disrespect for those he considered less able than him (his feud with Henry Dyer being exhibit one), and he has nothing bad to say anywhere about McVean. He has little good to say about him either, but then Brunton only seems to praise when it surprises him to find something worth praising such as Fujikura and Terashima, who he sees as diamonds in the rough.

ARCHIBALD WOODWARD BLUNDELL

Little is known about Blundell. He resigned along with McVean in September 1869 but stayed in place until May 1870 when his replacement, Stirling Fisher, arrived in Japan. In that time, he took over the Mikomotoshima Lighthouse supervision from McVean.

After leaving the lighthouse service, he worked on the railways in Japan until April 1876, leaving Japan with McVean and sailing to San Francisco on the *Belgie*. The McVeans took the train to Philadelphia and crossed the Atlantic from there, but Blundell stayed in the US, working in Colorado before effectively dropping off the map. An A W Blundell of San Francisco crops up in engineering journals and the like, but I was unable to categorically confirm that it was the same man. McVean and Blundell remained friends, corresponding for the rest of their lives.

13. *Omaezaki Lighthouse*

In 2007 Minori and I moved to Edinburgh. She wanted to improve her English and I wanted to see if Britain and I could get along. It didn't last. The economy was crashing and it took me nine months to get the offer of a permanent job, by which time my spirit had been broken. We just about saw the year out and returned to Japan, moving to Komaki, the next town over from Inuyama.

It wasn't great but it was convenient. We stayed there for eight years and have no friends from the town to show for it. They weren't the worst of times, but they weren't the best either. I experienced, for the first and, hopefully only time in my life, unemployment. It turns out I can't cope with a lack of direction and being financially reliant on anyone else. I went into a depression. My wife had a horrible job, and she went the same way. We had to get out but where?

Anywhere was the answer.

I applied for jobs in North America, across Asia. I nearly applied for a job in Kazakhstan. I regret not applying for it now; it was a great job. We also started looking for houses around Japan. We wanted our own place, settled, and a bit of land. A garden, some trees. It took three years of looking but we eventually found a place in Gifu. We moved in and it quickly turned out there was another British guy about half an hour's drive away.

A mutual friend introduced us, being the same age and British we engaged in the traditional ritual of drinking beer and talking about music. We hit it off, became friends. He got me a job at the university he worked at then quit (I should've taken that hint). As university teachers we get a stupid number of holidays. We teach for thirty weeks out of fifty-two. It's a hard life. It also means Ben and I are free a lot. Our wives work and his kids are in school, so during the vacations we meet for 'mornings'.

A 'morning' is a local custom where cafés and coffee shops serve a set breakfast, usually a boiled egg, a slice of toast, a little salad and a drink of your choice. It's the highlight of the day for the elderly. Coffee shops are stowed out. Ben and I have joined the ranks of the elderly and sit for hours chatting about our ailments over coffee refills.

I told him about this book and the trips I'd been making. My next trip was to Shizuoka where there was one lighthouse just about day-trippable. After one of our mornings, Ben opted to join me.

Ben and I have a lot in common: similar age, similar interests, we've both settled here, bought our houses and dug in for the long term. There's a divide between immigrants who are here for a few years and those of us who have committed. It expresses itself most obviously in friendships: Friends come and go. Even the best friendships may have a shelf life. When you're in the latter group it's a constant ripple running through interactions. How much should I invest in this? How much time does this friendship really have? It was Ben that articulated this to me, describing a sense of dread that gently haunts his life, a feeling that sooner or later everyone will get on a plane. As permanent emigrants, we have chosen a certain inevitable loneliness, but the choice doesn't make it any easier.

What to say about Shizuoka? The prefecture sits between Aichi (where Nagoya is) and the Kanagawa-Tōkyō hub; Mount Fuji stands astride Shizuoka's border with Yamanashi. Many of Japan's great historical figures either came from or spent a significant amount of their lives in Shizuoka. It's famous for green tea and...well, that's about it really. Of Japan's forty-seven prefectures, the *Lonely Planet Japan* has an entry for all but Shizuoka. Fuji is included as 'near Tōkyō'. A couple of towns are mentioned as day trips from Nagoya. If you ask locals for recommendations of places to visit in Japan, you'll get a long way down the list before Shizuoka City, Hamamatsu or Numazu are mentioned. If you push, then Gotemba might get the nod as a stop off on the way to Fuji from Tōkyō. Yet strangely, despite being constantly overlooked in recommendations, the Izu peninsula was and, to a significant extent still is, one of the most popular holiday destinations for Japanese people, boasting beaches, mountains and hot springs. One of my friends regularly goes there for the surfing, an eight-hour round trip to catch some waves. I begin to suspect a cover-up.

My research tells me there are three Brunton lighthouses still at work in Shizuoka: two of them at the bottom of the Izu peninsula and a third further west at Omaezaki.

Omaezaki is a two-and-a-half-hour drive and as always we fill that time talking mainly about music. We've reached that age where many people descend into that idiotic 'there's no good music out there anymore' old-man world. The music the kids listen to, it's all just noise. Ben and I are still exploring music, old and new, going forward into the brave new world of contemporary sounds and back to fill in the holes in our education. With age, I've found, has come an acceptance of wider quality. Bands that I dismissed on principle at university I have come to appreciate. The hip new tunes climbing the hit parade can still appeal to my old, wizened ears. Ben, however, has embraced technology much more, giving up solid-state music entirely in favour of streaming. I have no problem with streaming (I have huge problems with the main streaming companies) but I still prefer an artefact. The CD in my hand, a real record. Saying all that, both of us are on the cusp of falling into vinyl black holes. We are exactly the kind of morons to spend thousands on a turntable and to replace our entire collection with vinyl. So far, I've resisted the urge. So far.

We park below the lighthouse and climb the well-tended stairs. Here too, elderly people have congregated to paint watercolours of the lighthouse.

'Ask her for it,' Ben suggests. 'You can use it for the cover.'

I don't though. 'You know what manners here are like. If I ask she'll probably give it to me, even if she doesn't want to.'

Beside the lighthouse are a couple of souvenir shops. Ben has two daughters who love seashells so he gets a few polished pretty ones while I buy the inevitable postcards. The woman is chatty.

People are more talkative around Ben. He's smaller, slimmer than me, with an open, friendly face. My theory is that people find him non-threatening, whereas I, tall, broad, hairy, tend to warn people away from conversation. Ben and I can't spend long in a bar without him having a conversation with the person on the other side of him. In this case, a woman in her seventies, maybe eighties.

'Where are you from?'

'England,' says Ben, mischievously.

'Oh, I went to England years ago, in my twenties.' She wants to chat, so we take turns asking her about her trip to Europe. 'France and England. Paris and London. To be honest, I preferred Paris. I didn't feel safe in London. Too many black people.'

Right. We walk out. This is something you encounter reasonably often talking to older people in Japan, and it's pointless trying to address. It's taken as a non-controversial thing to say. She'll have told this story countless times to her friends and family and gotten a そうだね (I know what you mean) response each time. It's not racism to her, she'd be shocked if you described it as hate speech. She's merely reflecting her own preferences, the way you might discuss any matter of taste. It's a failure of the education system, which never raises these issues, and the media, which promote an 'us and them' outlook. Japanese uniqueness and the inherent hierarchy of humanity is a poisonous idea that sells newspapers and puts bums on seats. It's easier just to walk away.

Omaezaki is a tall one, overlooking a curve of headland. The shore isn't the prettiest, dark sand, lots of rocks, flotsam washed up. Fishermen and shellfish collectors. Work began in the middle of 1872 and it was illuminated 1 May 1874. You can get inside this one and even get a good look at the lamp, something that's usually and understandably shut off from tourists. We lean on the rails at the top, 22.5 m above ground, 54 m above the sea, looking out, chatting about nothing.

A sign near the entrance tells us that part of Kinoshita Keisuke's film *Shin Yorokobbimo Kanashimimo Ikutoshitsuki* (called *Times of Joy and Sorrow* in the US, *The Lighthouse* in the UK) was shot here. Another sign quotes some lyrics from the theme song, composed by Kinoshita Chuji. Neither of us have heard of the film or song, so we dutifully Google. *Times of Joy and Sorrow* it turns out is a film from 1957 about the difficult life of a lighthouse keeper and his wife. It was a huge success and has been remade under various titles three times (in 1986, 1997 and 2007). The song was a massive hit for

Wakayama Akira, a song that everyone of a certain age knows by heart. They used another of Brunton's lighthouses, Anorisaki, in the film, as well as eight others around the country. The song is about what you'd expect from the era, mournful, a strong male vocal with an almost military backing, it hasn't dated well but you can easily see some grandad belting it out at his local karaoke.

Back down, we take a wander along the path, stopping at various lookout points and a weird statue of a naked woman with seabirds on her head. We duck into a café for lunch and then head for home. Once again, lighthouses prove an excellent excuse to visit somewhere new, to get out and about with a good friend. A change is as good as a rest, they say, and there's little more invigorating than a sea breeze at the top of a lighthouse hitting you directly in the face. It makes the pulse quicken and the cells spark.

14. *The Science Bit*

It's impossible to prepare yourself for an earthquake. When you come to Japan you know they'll happen, and you imagine what that must be like, but your imagination isn't up to the task. No one's is. My first experience came soon after I arrived in 2005 when a mild tremor set me panicking and my students to laughter and mocking. Less funny were the minutes of shaking on 11 March 2011 when the Great East Japan Earthquake struck. To date I've been lucky enough to never experience that level of earthquake close up - this area is due, over 500 years due, but so far nothing.

All Brunton's education and apprenticeship was in Europe and Europe doesn't really do natural disasters, at least not recently. Or maybe I should say not yet. There's a reason we're all still so obsessed with Pompeii - there hasn't been much that big since. Earthquakes are possible. Occasionally you get them in England, usually around Birmingham for some reason, and then the news goes into overload, attempting to manufacture drama out of a student reporting they were woken a little after lunch by a mild jolt, or a woman saying her dog was startled. For all the Stevensons' brilliance, they hadn't really had to deal with earthquakes before.

While hunting for their man, the Stevensons got to work designing a system that would deal with earthquakes. Brunton was not impressed. In order to mitigate 'seismic disturbances', they traded away light efficiency:

> Metal reflectors were adopted instead of the much more powerful glass lenses, and the lanterns were made lower than usual, thus preventing their proper ventilation. A device was adopted of making a break in the rigidity of the structure, or what was termed an aseismatic joint.

Aseismatic joints were:

> spherical balls of bell-metal, working in cups of the same
> metal, placed between two platforms, the lower cups being
> fixed to the beams forming the foundation, and the upper
> cups being fixed to the lower beams of the superstructure,
> thus admitting free motion of the upper over the lower part
> of the building.

This was a waste of time as far as Brunton was concerned, and if
anything made the lighthouses weaker when faced with high winds.
The thinking was based on an assumption Brunton would later
prove wrong: that the shaking of the ground would increase up the
length up the lighthouse - the higher the lighthouse, the worse the
shaking at the top. In fact, the opposite is true:

> the slight elasticity of the materials of which they are constructed
> entirely absorbs the motion of the foundations by the time it
> reaches the summit...I had been on the balcony of a brick light-
> house, eighty feet above the ground, and had seen people
> immediately below me rush from their houses in panic on account
> of an earthquake shock, which I did not feel in the least.

In true Brunton style, he concludes that the great Messrs
Stevenson, accomplished and learned as they were, came to a wholly
erroneous conclusion. He even delivered these conclusions to
the Institute of Civil Engineers on 14 November 1876; George
Stevenson was president of the Institute of Civil Engineers at the
time. In that paper, 'The Japan Lights', he shows great awareness
of local architecture in withstanding earthquakes, a different and
more balanced view than the one expressed in his memoir about the
backwardness of the dwellings.

Work began on the first lighthouse - Mikomotoshima - in April
1869. Brunton travelled to Shimoda with McVean and his family to
break ground. McVean would remain there for three months, after
which he and Blundell rotated a month each until McVean packed

it in altogether. Mikomotoshima is, as he describes it, a solitary rock some seven miles off Shimoda Bay. It was the main route in and out of Yokohama (most shipping came from China and the rest of Asia, not the US) and stood as an enormous danger to passage. Therefore, it was top of the list.

This is perhaps where Brunton's education with the Stevensons most paid off. The Lighthouse Stevensons were experts at exactly this sort of work having conquered the Bell Rock. Bathurst's book of the same name does an unbeatable job of describing the astounding story of how they built a lighthouse on a rock which was mostly underwater, even at low tide, in the North Sea off the coast of Arbroath. The story of the men who died so that ships could, after thousands of years, avoid certain doom on the reef, is one I urge you to go and read. For our story it tells Brunton that this can be done. It had been done, on a rock far smaller and further from the coast than Mikomotoshima. Brunton was born near Arbroath, he grew up on the north-east coast. His father was in the Coastguard. The Bell Rock light is visible from the mainland. He didn't need mathematics to prove it could be done; he'd seen it with his own eyes. Standing on the shoulders of giants, as they say, the view is better.

Work progressed slowly, in part because of the difficulty of the job, and in part because of the paucity of craftsmen with the necessary skills and experience. Of highest importance was a mason, and McVean despaired at his resources. A British mason, J Marks, was hired and quickly put to work, yet he was but a single man.

One issue that slowed things down was the absence of decent bricks and a lack of brick-making skills. Mikomotoshima was built, in part, using bricks from Europe that had been used as ballast in the ships. Lime for mortar also caused problems. Iron was scarce and had to be imported, but wood was plentiful and of good quality. Local artisans needed to be educated in the techniques and the theory behind them, not just to erect lighthouses but to create good, reliable materials for all his projects. Over the course of 1869 Brunton hired, from Britain, a team of thirty-three blacksmiths, masons, carpenters and plumbers. Everything he needed had to be imported, but that couldn't last indefinitely.

There were willing and talented students, as Fujikura would go on to show, but Brunton had too much on his plate to begin apprenticeships (again, showing Fujikura's great luck at being at Brunton's side every day as his interpreter). By November 1870 the Japanese had opened a school teaching maths and engineering in Yokohama and 'a great rage for education set in'. It was this great rage that led to Fujikura and others being sent abroad to learn more, faster. Brunton writes that he received a pay raise for his efforts but beyond ordering books and instruments for study, his main energies lay elsewhere. It was for people like Henry Dyer to teach the first generation of Japanese civil engineers. Brunton had too much else to do.

Another area of constant innovation was with the lights themselves. Here Brunton would not run any risks and imported everything at increased expense, mainly from James Milne & Son and Dove & Co, both of Edinburgh. In advance, concerned about earthquakes, the Stevensons had decided on using reflector lights, rather than dioptric ones, as they are sturdier. For the same reason the lanterns were to be set low and be of increased strength. Brunton disagreed. While efforts were made to mitigate for earthquakes, Brunton was realistic about what would happen if the big one did strike.

> The whole country is subject to severe earthquakes; but that any single lighthouse should experience a shock of such severity as would derange its optical apparatus, is a remote contingency, and not likely to occur more than once a century. It may further be assumed, that such a shock as would fracture the apparatus would, in all probability prove destructive to the lighthouse tower in which it was placed.

In other words, we'll make preparations but if an earthquake hits a lighthouse, there's not a huge amount we can do about it beyond rebuilding afterward. To this end, spares were stored on site and in greater numbers in Yokohama. It's a pragmatism few who haven't experienced natural disasters can fully grasp. The people demanding the government 'do something' about Icelandic volcanic eruptions interrupting flight plans, or the Scottish rugby coach dismissing a typhoon as a bit of wind during the 2019 Rugby World Cup in Japan leap to mind. There's never much you can do beyond batten down the hatches and ride it out.

In his paper, 'The Japan Lights', Brunton points out the dioptric lights are cheaper, require less specialised skill to prepare and repair, and have fewer issues with intense heat and ventilation while consuming twenty-five per cent less oil. After the first tranche of lights was built, he got his way.

Oil was the big issue. In the days of electricity, it's easy to forget that these lights were literally *lit*. Every evening the keepers would climb to the top and put fire to wick. Japan has some fossil fuel resources but at this time they were not being exploited. Oil had to be imported. The first oil used was extracted from nuts in China (Brunton doesn't specify but it sounds like tung oil) however a regular supply was doubtful. Oil extracted from beans was tried next but the quality was 'variable', as was the case with other vegetable oils. Brunton favoured the Doty lamp, burning paraffin imported from Bathgate. He experimented with American kerosene which was much cheaper to import (forty-five to sixty cents per gallon compared with seventy-five) but it burned twenty-five per cent faster than paraffin negating the benefits. It is interesting to note that the Japanese for kerosene, 灯油 (tōyu) contains one of the same kanji (characters) as lighthouse (灯台 tōdai), and literally means 'oil for lamps' and is the principal oil used in heaters today. Brunton continued experimenting, refining and perfecting throughout his time in Japan, never settling, always improving. All of this experimentation would have been carried out on the practice lighthouse built in the yard at Yokohama. It's a real shame that none of that survived the mania for rebuilding.

15. *Inubōsaki Lighthouse*

Copper wire was invented by two Aberdonians fighting over a penny. So goes the old joke – a doubled-layered one, reinforcing the dual stereotypes of Scottish skinflintery and inventiveness.

I get a healthy research budget from the day job but when it comes time to spend it, I find myself hunting for bargains, cost-cuts and work-arounds. This is where I differ from some of my colleagues who subscribe to the idea that budgets are other people's money and therefore meant to be wasted. I'm more reticent, trying to justify each expense and decision.

This is how I came to be a regular guest at Commun Shibuya, a capsule hotel ten minutes from Shibuya Station in Tōkyō. The phrase 'capsule hotel' conjures images of plastic coffins ranked in rows like birth-pods or stasis booths in some science fiction film. Commun is a touch more upmarket, though the capsule itself is still somewhat coffinesque. Wood-lined rather than white plastic, and more spacious – I can actually sit up in there – and the facilities are stylish and clean. It's also incredibly cheap: 15,000 yen for three nights rather than 15,000 for one night around the corner. And it's within walking distance of Shibuya Station, a major hub and tourist site in Tōkyō. You know that famous crossing? Yeah, that's Shibuya.

I don't have a great record with capsule hotels. A few years back I came through to Tōkyō to meet my friend Zoë who was in town for an International PEN conference. She was staying in a nice hotel in Shinjuku and, being a skint language school teacher at the time, I opted for a capsule hotel, also in Shinjuku. I'd never stayed in one before and was a bit nervous about not having checked in and having to leave my bags in a locker by the station for the day, but the drink and karaoke soon made me forget my worries. At some ungodly hour of the morning Zoë went back to her hotel and I drunkenly made my way to the other side of Shinjuku Station, under overhead train lines, through side streets and around vomiting salarymen.

What I hadn't realised, and was now becoming painfully clear to me, was that not all parts of Shinjuku are equal. This part, Kabukichō, is the red-light district. I had to make my way by calls for 'massage' and 'girls'. I got to the hotel and checked in. I was handed pyjamas.

'I don't need these,' I said in Japanese.

'Yes, you have to wear them.'

I shrugged. How would they know in the capsule?

'You change here.'

'What?'

'You change here. Put all your belongings in the locker. Nothing in the capsule.'

I looked around and all the other men were doing the same. No women, obviously. I stripped down, changed quickly and put everything in the locker, making sure I kept my phone. The guy at the locker next to mine noticed my confusion.

'Yakuza.'

'Huh?'

'Tattoos. They check. No yakuza allowed.'

'Ah. Okay.' That made sense. Security in this area. Keep the outside out. I felt more relaxed, safer. The behaviour outside was frightful but inside was, if not delightful, then at least conducive to sleep when the only thing separating your bed from the world is a thin curtain. I traipsed downstairs to the capsules with the others. On the landing where the stairs turned, stood a heavily made-up young woman.

'Massage?'

'Massage? Really?'

She mimed a massage but her expression indicated anything but.

How? In a capsule? Massage or 'massage,' how is that physically possible? I realised that, in trying to work out the logistics, I'd stopped on the stairs. I was holding everyone else up while I was, it looked to them, either window shopping or negotiating. I quickly moved on, found my capsule and pulled the curtain tight. I looked around my pod.

How?

This weekend I'm in town for a conference paid for through my research budget. PLL3. Psychology of Language Learning. Plenary speakers include Zoltán Dörnyei and Ema Ushioda, rock stars in the field of motivation, an area of research I which I have a lot of interest. Ushioda is on Friday. Zoltán the Motivator is on Sunday. I decide to be a bit sneaky and slip out on the Saturday to pay a visit to Inubōsaki where Brunton's lighthouse is celebrating its 150th anniversary.

Inubōsaki is in Chiba Prefecture, a prefecture I have no other reason to ever visit. It's home to Tōkyō Disneyland and not a lot else. I've been to Tōkyō Disneyland once. Never again. If I don't take advantage of my current proximity to Inubōsaki, I'll have to make the trip back and that'll cost a lot of my money. My reticence about spending other people's money only goes so far.

Somehow, through being over-organised and a country boy in the big city, I manage to get to Tōkyō Station, thirty minutes from Shibuya, an hour before the first train to Choshi leaves. At this time nothing in the station is open save for souvenir shops. If you want to buy boxes of Tōkyō Banana or senbei, the choice is startling. Coffee? Nope.

Japan has an odd relationship with coffee, particularly if you are a tourist here. Hotel rooms will have a kettle, cups and six different kinds of tea, but no coffee. Not even some shitty instant one-cup pouch. But there will be a free coffee machine in the lobby. Like coffee is something you only drink while waiting to check in.

My worst experience was at a ryokan in Takayama. We went down for breakfast, were seated, and Minori realised she had forgotten something, so quickly ran back to the room. The older woman serving us came to take our drink order. I ordered Minori's tea and asked if they had coffee - asked, didn't presume - all in Japanese.

Silence.

I ask again.

She doesn't even look at me, just walks away.

Minori comes back.

The woman comes back. Again, without looking at me, she says to Minori, in Japanese, 'I'm really sorry but we don't have coffee'.

Minori, not having been here for the interaction, has no idea what she's talking about, and says so.

'The foreigner wants coffee but we don't have any.'

I'm getting pretty angry. Minori says, 'Why are you telling me?'

I say, in Japanese, 'I asked you. Why did you walk away? And now, why are you talking to my wife and not to me?' I have raised my voice.

She finally turns to me and says, in big, exaggerated English, 'COFFEE. NO!'

Minori can already see that the day is ruined.

I say, 'I'm speaking to you in Japanese. Why won't you speak to me in Japanese?'

Nothing. She walks off. I hear her say to someone else, 'The foreigner is angry because we don't have coffee'.

The train arrives and I fall asleep, missing every inch of the landscape for the two hours it takes to Choshi. I wake, dazed, at the terminus and find the Choshi Electric Railway, a quaint ye olde style trainline that winds through the hills and, seemingly, in and out of people's gardens. Inubō is the second to last stop, a bizarre station decked out like the fever-dream of some Hollywood idea of a Latin American town square.

I walk alongside a group of elderly hikers layered up in professional mountain gear despite the already intense heat and the fact that we're only going ten minutes along the side of a major road. It's all about the gear here. Take up a sport, even for a day, and you need all the gear. They'll have camping stoves, military-grade GPS, the works. We take a left, a right, and behind the hideous, faded, salmon-pink of the apparently abandoned Marine Park the lighthouse appears. To the right, the south, the cliff drops sharply to a rocky shore where the obligatory fishermen perch on the limits, already well into their stock of beers. A walking path winds along the shoreline which eventually turns into a golden-brown sandy beach backed by a couple of hotels. The lighthouse sits on a promontory. To the north the beach continues and a handful of paddle boarders bob on the calm water. A row of souvenir shops and cafés that have seen better days advertise the usual snacks and ice creams. Draught beer too, but I don't have the excuse of the fishermen. It's not even eleven yet.

The car park is filling up and the top deck of the lighthouse is packed with silhouettes looking back at me. I walk all the way around the perimeter of the lighthouse. At the back there is what looks like a radar station, whether weather or Coastguard is unclear, but the spiky tower and sweeping bar emit a low-level high-pitched whine that is off-putting and unsettling. I don't dwell on the clifftops and pay the 200-yen entry fee.

The original cottages remain intact and one has been turned into a museum packed with machinery and lamps. A cast iron bell stands proud in the yard and photos of some of Brunton's other lighthouses hang from a white-washed wall.

It being the 150th anniversary of the illumination, there is a photo contest being advertised with big cash prizes. I focus my attention a bit more on the snaps I'm taking. Usually, I just catch everything treating the framing as an afterthought in the quest to record and research. With 100,000 yen on offer, I take a bit more time. It would be a nice coda to the book to announce a win. Of course, as soon as I leave, I forget all about it and never enter. Spoiler.

The ground floor of the lighthouse has been turned into another museum, this one with an impressive bust of Brunton. It's unclear at what point in his life this was made and whether he sat for it. His mutton chop whiskers are there but so is an impressively receding hairline of the Clive Anderson variety. Brunton was twenty-six when he came to Japan, thirty-five when he left, so Japan never saw him as an old man. He died aged fifty-nine, so in some respects no one saw him as an old man.

Work began on the lighthouse at the start of 1872 and it was illuminated on 15 November 1874. It stands 31.3 m high (52.3 m above sea level) and was the first lighthouse constructed entirely through domestically produced brick, meaning by 1872 Brunton was more than satisfied with the production line he'd created. This would no doubt save a lot of money and logistical headaches.

Inubōsaki Lighthouse

I climb to the gallery and enjoy the beautiful view along the coast. Compared to some others, the information here is sparse and there is nothing, um, illuminating. I climb back down, pressing myself into the wall when people come the other way, a frequent occurrence on this summery Saturday. I buy yet another phone strap, a plastic file and a couple of postcards, and an ice cream which I mostly get in my beard, something a helpful cyclist points out. But the lighthouse done, there's little else to do here. I go back to the station, putter back to Choshi and discover that the next high-speed train doesn't leave for another three-and-a-half hours. I clamber onto the local train that will take me to Tōkyō, eventually, via every other town in Chiba, just as my phone battery dies. No more music, no more podcasts. No internet. Thankfully, I have a good old-fashioned paperback with me, Chang-rae Lee's *On Such a Full Sea*, which I picked up last year in Seoul, a book I am enjoying but which

Ursula Le Guin had little time for. I settle in for hours of dystopia and gently-rocking carriages. The lighthouse in Chiba is checked off and I never need return, but I can't help thinking, as hundreds of junior high school students push into the carriage, that a seven-hour round trip is a bit much. Perhaps I should have gone to the conference on motivation after all.

16. *1869*

Building was underway. Each lighthouse required different materials depending on location, purpose, local resources and budget. Brick, stone, wood and iron were all used, but there is a definite Brunton style:

> They are generally circular at the base, and the walls have a straight batter on the outside, and are plumb on the inside. Forming a semicircle round the bases are two store-rooms, one for oil, and the other for dry stores. Paint, fuel, and additional store-rooms are erected on the grounds. The lightkeeper's dwellings are of stone and brick, and contain from six to eight rooms: the kitchens and outhouses are in separate buildings. The grounds are surrounded by a stout fence of wall, about 8 feet high.

As always with Brunton, this design was the subject of some heated discussion. Given the difficulty in communicating and travelling within Japan, Brunton felt that a minimum of one year's stores should be kept on site but the latest in the revolving door of superiors at this time, Sano, thought six months' would be sufficient. With Parkes outside Japan at that time his usual tactic of going over the officer's head was closed. Instead he just ignored Sano's instructions.

> Sano, on discovering it, he ordered that one half...was to be returned. On my pointing out the practical impossibility of doing do, Sano became quite indignant, as he said, at being forced to acquiesce in what he had decided against; but made no further objection.

Years later, Brunton notes, Sano apologised for the way he had tried to manage Brunton, justifying yet another piece of 'harmless deception' on Brunton's part.

1869 was a busy year for Brunton and the lighthouse team. In addition to the lighthouses, the survey of Yokohama was ongoing; it would be concluded at the end of April, just before Blundell left the service. There was a flurry of memos and reports flying from Brunton's desk: new staff had to be hired in Britain and sent over along with whatever materials couldn't be found nearby. Explanations and rules concerning how to work the lights and man the lighthouses had to be written and translated into Japanese. Local lighthouse keepers had to be found and trained. To that end, a full explanation of the lighthouse establishment rules and practices from the Northern Lighthouse Board (developed by the Stevensons) had to be translated. There were railways and telegraphs; a renovation of the British embassy; recommendations for the settlement. A ship had to be bought to tender the lighthouses and a captain found for it.

To this end a ship was purchased. Called in Japanese 灯明丸 (Tōmyō Maru, transliterated as Tōmei in some sources but I go with the Yokohama Archives) which simply means 'torch ship', it was known as the *Sunrise* to all. The idea was that it would move construction materials and lighthouse supplies, as well as maintain the light buoys, ships and beacons, and mean they were independent (they'd needed to borrow the *Manilla* from the Navy to make the first survey trip). Of course, that independence had to be jealously guarded. Ueno Kagenori, finally returned overland from Nagasaki, became Brunton's 'superior officer' and 'he once again took up his somewhat erratic and always obstructive direction of lighthouse affairs'. Ueno 'sought at once to divert' the *Sunrise*, and the two fought over the issue. Ueno, who would rise far up the diplomatic pyramid and would go on to become Consul to Great Britain was a man used to having his way. His portrait shows a confident young man, one not afraid of a fight, sure of his place in the world. That place was over mere mortals and particularly over foreigners like Brunton. Brunton, railing against this brick wall, went to Parkes who in turn went over Ueno's head. In the meantime, the original owner refused to hand over the boat until it had been fully paid for. The tone Brunton takes suggests this may have been a ruse – the owner had the first instalment of $15,000 (out of $60,000) – since without a crew of his own, Ueno was powerless to move the ship an inch. By the time the full amount was paid the idea of using the ship for anything other than its intended purpose was quietly dropped.

Brunton hired Albert Brown as captain of his new ship. Brown had worked for P&O and was captain of the *Aden* when Brunton sailed to Japan. He took command on 24 February with 'English officers and engineers, with a native crew'. Brunton had a lot of respect for Brown who, after aiding in the survey of Yokohama Bay, went on to survey many more bays around Japan.

On 7 July, they took the *Sunrise* on its first survey trip, returning to Satamisaki where weather and rough seas had postponed the survey the previous year. This time they could make a landing, though not everyone managed it:

> The Satsuma officers on their arrival made the attempt to land on the rock to join me, but failed. In making the attempt, their boat was in great risk of being swamped, while one or two of them were in such a state of collapse from seasickness, that they were incapable of movement.

Brunton seems to have enjoyed this trip immensely, relishing his time with the 'Prince' of Satsuma and meeting Dr William Willis, who then lived in Satsuma. He also enjoyed the company of his Japanese companion 'Inouye' (Inoue) who he describes as having 'imbibed all the sense of humour and restless energy of the American people, among whom he was educated...he poured out undiluted ridicule on the antiquated methods of his compatriots, and startled them by the vigour of his methods'. It should be noted here that the Yokohama Archives state that Ueno was the one who made this trip with Brunton but this seems unlikely: Brunton struck up a real friendship with Inoue, who was in the audience in 1878 when Brunton presented 'The Japan Lights' to the Institute of Civil Engineers. That said, his memoir does contain a number of mistakes, inaccuracies and impossibilities and as we have seen, much of what he claims was conjecture and biased assumptions. Still, it seems unlikely that a memory as strong as this one seems to be (we get much more detail about this trip than the previous one) could be false. If Brunton had spent a month travelling with Ueno, there would be pages and pages of complaints.

The *Sunrise*, however, would quickly prove insufficient for their purposes: they were going to need a bigger boat. In April 1870 the *Thabor*, a steamer with a paddle wheel, was purchased from a French company though not without some objection from the government who had just bought Brunton a ship. Brunton, realising that he personally might be the problem here, took a step back and asked Parkes to negotiate in whatever way he saw best. It was a rare moment of pragmatism in the face of bureaucracy, and it worked. Thirteen months after taking delivery of the *Sunrise*, the *Thabor* was his.

That wasn't the end of the matter. Yokohama, unsurprisingly, was home to corruption and by cutting out any agents when negotiating the sale, he had robbed these men of their chance of a hefty fee. A rumour got round that Brunton himself had acted as broker and pocketed $10,000 in the process and Brunton was the subject of much gossip at the Yokohama Club and a visit to his house at 4 am by 'a busy-body'. Both Parkes and the Japanese government were happy that Brunton wasn't on the make. When it came to lightships (a boat that acts as a lighthouse, they are used where a lighthouse is impractical or impossible) it was decided it would be much easier to build their own.

The *Sunrise* did have a secondary use, though, in rescuing ships that had come to mischief. The most dramatic of these was when the *Bombay* and *Oneida* collided off Yokohama. The *Oneida* sank with the loss of all 110 men. The *Sunrise* was tasked with finding the wreck and marking it with a buoy, though given the depth of the ocean there, this was eventually deemed unnecessary.

Staffing was a major headache throughout 1869, not least because of McVean and Blundell's resignations in September. Brunton was getting annoyed at the constant carousel of supervisors, men who were not specialists and were on their way elsewhere, attention divided. Ueno was soon gone, and in all Brunton had to deal with fifteen overseers, presumably having to bring each up to speed. I'd imagine by 1876 he had his welcome briefing down pat.

Another necessary appointment was for an accountant. As with Brown, Brunton turned to someone he already knew, in this case his brother-in-law, George Wauchope. What Eliza's parents thought about their son-in-law shipping three of their six children out to Japan is not recorded. George would spend the rest of his life in Japan and is buried in Yokohama. Mary, Eliza's sister, would remain in Japan too, marrying Edwin Bruges Watson.

This wasn't the biggest problem of the year. While some materials could be sourced and others replicated on site, the actual lights themselves had to be ordered and imported. On 10 December 1869 the *Elleray* sank off the coast of Taiwan (Formosa, as it was known then) taking the lights down with it. The delay caused by placing another order forced Brunton to improvise temporary lights. He commissioned copper lamps from Japanese artisans, bought lenses more usually meant for shipboard use, and by grouping these together could make a light powerful enough for the time being. He also imported the kind of lights used on American trains. These temporary lights were put on wooden towers in the most dangerous spots.

It was the custom at the time for a 'Notice to Mariners' to be published giving details of the lights so that sailors could be sure of their trustworthiness. Brunton expected his name to adorn the notice but his superiors were reluctant to publicly acknowledge that a foreigner was responsible. A compromise was reached whereby his chief (whoever that happened to be that week) would be named, with Brunton as 'Engineer' coming in second place.

On 26 November Brunton attended a meeting of the Yokohama Residents to explain his plans for the sewerage system and in December Yoshida Bridge opened for traffic. Around this time Brunton's second daughter, Harriet, was born in Yokohama. All in all, a productive year.

17. *Nabeshima Lighthouse*

After a Christmas Day of wine and jazz in Kōbe, Minori and I wake with Boxing Day hangovers to find it pissing down. We spend a quiet breakfast complaining about the state of the sausages, desperate for coffee but knowing there'll be none until we can find a Starbucks drive-thru. I get the car, pull a U-turn across four lanes of traffic and we're finally heading in the right direction. Okayama Prefecture, and another lighthouse.

Steaming, literally, down the highway with 3 Colours Red blasting the blues away, tunnel after tunnel. I hate driving through tunnels, there's something hypnotic, something that sends me drifting away, drifting across lanes. It's an Isaac Asimov thing, caves of steel, enclosed megacities with mindless automata suddenly turning on you, or maybe an Arthur C Clarke thing, *Space Odyssey* star travel, a kaleidoscope and speeded up footage of the Grand Canyon.

Suddenly we burst onto the Setobashi, the Great Seto Bridge, the longest dual-level suspension bridge in the world. I had prepared jokes about it not being a patch on the Forth Bridge but when the final tunnel pulled back and two huge suspension towers emerged from the fog before disappearing into the clouds, I was so awestruck I took my foot off the gas, coasting onto this feat of civil engineering. Minori says it looks like something out of *Star Wars* and I know what she means. The scale of it is otherworldly. It's hard to imagine a bunch of blokes doing this.

The problem with that, I say, is that civil engineering of this scale in SF usually has prison or death at the end, or at least a psycho in a cape and helmet waiting to tell you his plan in the weird formal English bad writers think everyone uses in the future. It isn't helped by the smoking power plant at the end of it all. It curves, each leg resting on an island or a block so ridiculous in scale that you wonder if there were indeed giants roaming the Earth, as the *Bible* tells us.

The moody sky, the battering wind, a setting that could only be CGI, I can feel myself becoming a little unhitched. Are we really in Japan? Did the tunnel take us to another dimension? A parallel universe? I've long been fascinated by that idea. Journeys to the centre of the Earth, passageways, tunnels that lead elsewhere. As writers there are ideas, tropes, metaphors that we keep coming back to and this is one of mine. When you can no longer see the sky, anything is possible.

Nabeshima is one of the islands supporting this 'Iain Banksian' Bridge, and one of Brunton's lighthouses shares a corner. Wikipedia says it's extinguished but Japanese websites assure me that's not the case, just the light has been updated a few times and was fully automated in the 1990s.

It's technically in Kagawa Prefecture, a new one for me. The satnav is giving us hassle, refusing to do what it's told, so we pull off the highway, down the helter-skelter into the parking area to sort out where we're going and for the obligatory 'there's a toilet so I might as well use it' stop. Ah, age.

It's just as well we did stop. The reason the satnav cannot cope is that this is the end of the road. Only locals are allowed to drive onto Nabeshima. None shall pass. From here we have to walk. Umbrellas and raincoats out, not that it matters. It's raining and humid at the same time, so we'll get wet regardless. The lighthouse is on a tiny island called Nabeshima because it looks like an upturned pan (nabe = pan). It's linked to the mainland by a bridge. From the map in the parking area it looks far. The rain is getting heavier. Why did we think doing this on Boxing Day was a clever idea? We're going shopping later. Maybe I can just curl up in the lighthouse and sleep.

We follow the path to a dead end, eventually spotting a little gap in the fence with an arrow pointing under the bridge. I'm glad Minori is with me, I'd probably have given up at this point, but dragging her all this way to then give up just before the goal...We squeeze through and follow the narrow path downhill, terrified of slipping.

It's another island like Sugashima; not quite as dilapidated but on the same trajectory. Abandoned houses, overgrown. Walls in danger of falling down. Something in the air, decay perhaps. There are no jobs here, little to offer beyond fishing or a long commute every day, so the young leave, the old die, and that's the end of things. There are communities like it all over Japan. I knew, intellectually, they were here but without this project I'd probably never have seen them. Why else would you visit Nabeshima if not for the lighthouse? Sugashima? Tomogashima? Forgotten corners of the country, with forgotten people still holding on. This is what it means to be a nation, to be part of something larger, to be part of a world economy: as things scale up, the small gets lost. Coming from a small country that's forced to remain part of something larger, I know how that feels. Too big to fail? So big, failure is guaranteed. We need to rethink, reset, scale it back. Cosmopolitan but small, a union of parts, not subsumed into a whole, but a team, individuals working together.

Maybe it's the hangover. Maybe it's the weather. Maybe it's the decay of Nabeshima. We wind through streets only wide enough for two people to pass at an angle. We've lost all sense of direction, of intention. There's no horizon in these ruined streets. Finally, it opens out. We've reached the far side, completely crossed the island and gone too far. Rather than retracing our footsteps we follow the coast round. The bridge we'd seen on the map is actually a harbour wall,

Nabeshima Lighthouse

enclosing a little fishing fleet. The far end, the little islandette where they built the lighthouse is behind a fence and a locked gate. We can just see the top of it over the trees. While I'm taking photos – moody black-and-white, of course – Minori crosses to the gate. A sign says 'No Entry' but she fiddles with it for a minute and gets it open.

'Was it locked?'

'Yes, but not very well.'

We follow the steps up a twisting path, quickly coming out at the top.

It's a short one; looking out over the Inland Sea it doesn't need to be visible from far away. Squat, light in the middle, support building either side. Symmetrical. I go through the usual routine, photos, rock, touch. There's a CCTV camera but I doubt anyone is watching. We head back down, back through the little streets and back to the car, miserable, soaking.

We head next to Kurashiki, an old town converted into a shopping district. All the old buildings remain, the beautiful canal through the centre. Some of the shops are for souvenirs, some for local crafts, some just for fashion. We dry off, wander around, eat sanitised street food, buy chopstick rests and saké cups. Over lunch we realise the Ohara Museum of Art has an extensive collection of Saeki Yuzo's works. Not the biggest – his hometown of Osaka is building a new gallery that will house some fifty-six paintings – but more than the few in Wakayama and the odd one or two scattered throughout the country. In the gallery we buy a canvas replica of his 'Verdun' which hangs behind my desk, visible whenever I do Zoom events at home.

It's hard to say why Saeki has become our adopted painter. Perhaps it's the style: heavily influenced by European impressionism but putting his own spin on things. Perhaps it's the subject matter: French alleys, Parisian cafés, the kinds of images I worshipped as a romantic adolescent poet. I had the honour of staying for two nights in the Shakespeare and Company bookstore in Paris when I was twenty, and it is still one of the things I am most delighted by in my life. Waking up to the bells of Notre Dame, surrounded by books, in the bookshop that published *Ulysses*, run at that time by George

Whitman who showed me his first edition of *Ulysses*, who made me pancakes, who shouted at me for wasting water when I did his dishes. It's my dream to go back one day as a writer, to read there. I could die happy then. So perhaps that's why Saeki appeals to me: a shared romantic view of Paris and art.

Perhaps it's the biography. A man who never felt comfortable at home, who had to leave to grow into himself, who found his inspiration elsewhere, in exile, at home lost in a different language, a different culture. Saeki died aged thirty of TB, all but destitute, in a psychiatric hospital after a breakdown brought on by overwork and poverty. He's described by some as the Japanese Van Gogh, partly because of his style, partly because of his tragic end. Michael Brenson writing in the *Japan Times* describes him as writing in the void between Eastern and Western traditions, so perhaps that's the appeal for us, a family combining East and West. There's something in Saeki's almost illegible signs that speaks to us as bilingual with each other but not fluent with the world, people often lost in the other's culture, fascinated, attracted, but never fully integrated.

18. *Brunton's Other Trips*

Brunton made many surveying trips around Japan though he barely mentions them. In June 1871 he travelled along the Japan Sea coast to Niigata where the Shinano River was blocked to shipping by a sand bar. Niigata was a treaty port and needed to be opened, but the river was shallow in places and prone to flooding. The local government had dug channels in a bid to divert flood water but this had the unintended side effect of increasing the size of the sand bar. Having studied similar problems in Europe, Brunton decided that the river needed to be focused and narrowed so that the sand bar would be 'scoured' by the natural flow of water. As expected, the governor of Niigata disagreed with Brunton's plan, particularly the part where they stop the work already begun on side channels, but eventually 'light began to dawn on their minds' and he got to work on a full report.

In August 1871, now back in Yokohama, he received permission from Tōkyō and sent two of the new intake of assistants, Fisher and Wilson, to do a full survey. By March 1872, however, with the survey complete, work still had not begun and no response could be got from Niigata. The project resurfaced when Parkes wrote to Brunton in April 1873 passing on the news that a Dutch engineer was being hired to survey the Shinano River. It seemed Fisher's report had disappeared into the bureaucratic system and few even knew it had been done. Brunton notes that in 1875 the government finally decided to follow his plans but by then there was no money for the scheme.

Later in 1871 Brunton escorted some of the top government officials as well as Parkes, and W G Howell, the owner and editor of *The Japan Weekly Mail*, on the *Thabor* to Kōbe and then on to Osaka for the official opening of the new Mint. Brunton took the opportunity on the way there and back to sail them by his lighthouses, stopping at one or two for a bit of mild showing off.

Unlike Satow and Bird, Brunton is a poor source for information about Japanese scenery, culture or people. The only other trips that he dwells on are those to Okinawa (to which I will return later) and Taiwan (Formosa as it was at the time).

The title he chose for chapter twenty-two, 'The Expedition to Formosa', doesn't quite encapsulate the momentous event Brunton witnessed from the side lines. This was, in effect, an invasion by the Japanese and marks the first time the Japanese Imperial Army and Navy were deployed overseas.

A merchant ship from Okinawa (Ryūkyū as it then was) with a crew of sixty-six was wrecked off the coast of Taiwan. Local 'savages' as Brunton calls them, indigenous Paiwanese, beheaded fifty-four of them. The remaining twelve were rescued by Qing Chinese officials (Taiwan at the time was part of the Qing dynasty) and returned to Japan via China.

After demanding compensation and swift justice from the Chinese authorities and receiving neither, Japan, Brunton reports, decided to 'punish the murderers, and to sack and burn their towns and villages'. The problem was that the nascent Navy had no one who could navigate the unsurveyed waters around Taiwan. Captain Brown, who knew the waters well, volunteered to act as guide. Since Britain was not at war with China and had no desire to start one, Parkes stepped in and Brown was threatened with legal consequences should he take part in a military campaign against an ally. Brown ignored him and boarded the *Kuroda*, a civilian vessel requisitioned to function as a troop carrier. The owners turfed him off. He tried again and was evicted a second time. The military, keen on his experience, threw their weight around and Brown got his way. All this behind Parkes's back.

Brunton reproduces an amusing letter from Parkes asking for an update on Brown's location. Apparently, Brown had told Parkes he was off to Amoy (Xiamen, China) but Parkes received 'certain information' hinting at the truth. Brunton doesn't record his reply to this letter, whether he covered for his captain or not, but when Brown returned he was treated as a hero by the Japanese, given a significant raise in salary and other special honours. He ended up as

'Honorary Japanese Consul at Glasgow, superintending the completion of the numerous vessels constructed in that port for Japan'.

The expedition itself was declared a success. The Paiwanese were 'punished' though they fought something of a guerrilla campaign against the invaders, killing some Japanese and necessitating reinforcements. The biggest battle was with malaria, which wiped out at least 550 Japanese soldiers over the summer. By November the Qing government agreed to pay an indemnity and the Japanese left.

While the events of invasion aren't particularly noteworthy, their implications had long echoes through history. The Imperial Army and Navy had successfully deployed overseas, and this gave them the confidence to do it again, and experience from which to learn (for example, get good charts and navigators so you don't have to rely on adventurous Scots to get you to the battlefield). The incident confirmed Japan's control over Okinawa (which, as the Ryūkyū Kingdom had remained technically independent, playing Japan and China off against each other) although that would take some years to be acknowledged in international law. It also exposed China's lack of control over Taiwan and its lack of military strength. In 1894 Japan would successfully launch a war against China, beginning an occupation of Taiwan that would last until the end of World War Two. The First Sino-Japanese War of 1894-5 led to the 1904-5 war with Russia, the 1910 annexation of Korea, increasing expansion into China and involvement in World War One as a British ally. The Treaty of Versailles recognised Japanese colonial gains in China and that was the ballgame. What might have happened over the ensuring decades had Brown listened to Parkes?

19. *Nosappumisaki Lighthouse*

I'd happily live in Hokkaido but Minori won't countenance the winters. During summer though, Hokkaido is the place to be: a few degrees cooler than the rest of Japan, wide open spaces, mountains and lakes, great beer and whisky…I could almost be home.

I've been to Hokkaido a few times. The first trip was in 2005. I spent three nights in Sapporo which included a lock-in at a bar and some roast venison courtesy of a Dutch chef. The second time was for a conference in Otaru that climaxed on the Saturday night with us drinking all the beer in a local bar before getting stuck into the single malt back at the hotel. I don't think anyone made the Sunday presentations. I know I didn't. Hokkaido holds many fond memories.

Nosappumisaki Lighthouse

Francis was my first friend in Japan. We shared the same flight out from Heathrow, worked for the same company, found our feet here together, met our wives here. He returned to Derby with Ayaka and set about spawning, a state of affairs which guarantees a family trip to Nagoya at least once a year to see the in-laws. Grandparents means babysitters, so Francis gets a few days break to hang with his friends, while Ayaka does the same. Usually Francis comes to mine, we light the fire, crank the tunes and crack a bottle or two. This time, he's got the old wanderlust so, me being me, I suggest Hokkaido. He thinks lamb barbecue, the Sapporo brewery. I mean the Nosappumisaki Lighthouse at the far eastern edge of Hokkaido.

We get an early morning flight, pick up the rental car from the airport and hit the road. It's thirty-seven degrees in Nagoya so we expect Hokkaido to be about twenty-five degrees; perfect summer weather for two Brits. That's what we get in Sapporo, but as we head east the temperature drops, the rain starts. By the time we reach Lake Akan Ainu Kotan, our first stop, a thick fog has descended. We are not dressed for this. An adult life spent in Japan has robbed me of the Scottish habit of planning for four seasons in one day.

Lake Akan Ainu Kotan is a mixture of tourist site and historical site. The Ainu are the original people of this archipelago, the indigenous population. It is thought that the people who would become the Japanese nation, the Yamato-jin as they are known, migrated over from Korea while the Ainu would have migrated from what is now Russia; south-up and north-down, in other words. When these two groups met, it didn't end well for the Ainu who were increasingly limited to Hokkaidō, then not part of Japan. There was peaceful trade and violent encounters between the thirteenth and eighteenth centuries. In the nineteenth century the Tokugawa Bakufu took a more active stance, assuming control of Hokkaido and inflicting the kinds of policies on the Ainu that become all too familiar when you read the history of oppressed people: kidnap, forcible marriage, rape, indentured servitude and, of course, smallpox. Language and culture were trampled on, forced assimilation the norm, sudden, massive drops in population numbers.

In 1868, when the Meiji Restoration brought about political realignment and a reorganisation of the entire nation from feudal domains into the forty-seven prefectures we know today, Hokkaidō was officially brought into the fold. In 1899 all Ainu were granted full Japanese citizenship, effectively eradicating the idea of the Ainu as a separate people and setting the stage for the 'homogeneous' lie politicians trot out today. It was only in 2008 that the government passed a non-binding resolution that recognised the Ainu as an indigenous people of Japan, and it wasn't until 2019 that they became officially recognised under the constitution. Assimilation was so effective that today it is unknown how many Ainu there are in Japan with estimates ranging from 25,000 to 200,000. A survey in 2017 found only 13,000 people who identify as Ainu but because many still fear discrimination it's thought they hide their ancestry and lie on census forms.

The museum at Lake Akan makes my blood boil with indignation. It makes my petty complaints about micro-aggressions and bureaucratic discrimination pale into nothing. Here is a story as shocking as that of the Native Americans, the First Peoples, the Maori and Aborigines, but few outside Japan have ever heard of the Ainu and few in Japan care enough to learn anything about them. I am thankful that in my lifetime Scotland had the sense to reverse policies aimed at eradicating Scots and Gaelic language and culture (I come from a generation that were punished in school for saying 'aye' and lived to see dual-language signage across the country). A traditional Ainu dance was going to be included in the 2020 Olympic Opening Ceremony but was dropped because there wasn't room, even though space was found for dances based on manga and video games. Instead, it was performed in Sapporo in 2021 where the marathon was staged.

I buy an Ainu wall hanging that is meant to keep demons from your door and it currently hangs in my entranceway, a huge square of purple material with symmetrical geometric and curved patterns. While paying we chat in Japanese with an old Ainu man standing by the door next to a giant taxidermised bear, at least half as tall as me again, mouth an angry roar, claws drawn. He tells us he has seen many bears around here in his life but many more recently as development destroys their habitat. He is understandably saddened by this, rather than fearful. 'This is their home,' he says. 'We live here with their permission.' Then he laughs, points at my unkempt beard which is getting to Karl Marx proportions. 'You look like Ainu.'

The plan is to stay at a cheap guesthouse that night, get some beers and food, hopefully chat to some more local people, and then in the morning continue to the coast and see the lighthouse. Hokkaido has other ideas: the guesthouse is run down and in the middle of nowhere (even for Hokkaidō) so we have to drive to get dinner, and the weather is worsening. We buy a few cans and have an early night.

The next morning, the fog is so thick we can't see the car from the room, about 4 or 5 m away. We pack up and, partly due to foolish optimism but mainly because we can't think of anything else, head for a viewpoint above Lake Mashan and for the briefest of seconds see water. One of the most beautiful lake views in Japan is concealed behind clouds so thick you could stand on them. After shivering in our thin summer clothes and laughing at our lot, we get back in the car already knowing what to expect at Nosappumisaki.

What we don't expect are trilingual road signs in Japanese, English and – not Ainu – Russian. Geographically we're close to Russia up here and there are cruises to Vladivostok from Japan (on the list) but relations aren't good, so the signs are surprising. Russia and Japan are technically still at war: the Soviet Union declared war with Japan on 8 August 1945, after Hiroshima but before Nagasaki, and just a week before the surrender. It was basic opportunism as the Soviet Union invaded Karafuto/South Sakhalin and the Kuril Islands that lie between Hokkaidō and Kamchatka and then successfully claimed them at Yalta. They are useful strategically, guaranteeing access from the port at Vladivostok to the Pacific without passing through anyone else's territory, and still part of Russia today. Japan wants them back. Russia says no. As a result, the two nations have never signed a peace treaty and therefore are technically still at war. Hence my surprise at the road signs as we pass through Nemuro, the most eastern city in Japan.

Less surprising are the 'give us our islands back' banners around the lighthouse, or the typhoon-like winds barrelling across the roads threatening to send the rental car into the fields. We are really not dressed for this.

Work is being done on the roads around the lighthouse so we have to park at a nearby restaurant and walk. But no! The paths are closed too. We've come all this way and the signs tells us we can go no further. I can see the lighthouse but that's not enough: I've touched them all so far, even the ones behind fences. What would Minori do?

I climb over the fence onto the cliff top and, wind whipping around me, pick my way through the long grass and mud, keeping an eye out for snakes, landslides, holes, anything that could kill me in seconds.

We're really not dressed for this.

Francis shrugs and follows.

We make it, take some photos, and start laughing at the stupidity of it all. Workmen are sheltering in the cabs of their diggers and trucks, and we're here in shorts and t-shirts, scrambling along a clifftop in a howling gale and thick fog to see a lighthouse.

'It'll make a good story,' Francis says.

We head back to the gift shop where I buy whatever lighthouse stuff they have and a 'Wild North' bumper sticker for my car. The elderly woman behind the counter doesn't bat an eyelid at these two foreign idiots dressed like Vincent and Jules from *Pulp Fiction* after the Wolf has bailed them out. The utter lack of surprise somehow makes the whole thing funnier.

'Now what?'

'We might as well head back to Sapporo.'

'Ditch the car. Have a proper drink.'

'Sold.'

Soaked, freezing, we get in the car for the five-hour drive back.

Nosappumisaki is the event horizon of this project, the moment of no return, the point where I knew I was going to see this through no matter what: I'd made it to one of the remotest parts of Japan in ridiculous weather and didn't regret a second of it. Mikomotoshima, Kinkasan, lighthouses halfway to Korea? Bring it on.

146

20. *On Leave*

Things continued much the same for Brunton: lighthouses went up and were turned on, buoys and beacons were laid. Memos were issued, reports submitted, men hired and replaced. In November 1871 Brunton, along with some of his peers, was summoned to Tōkyō for an audience with the Emperor. The ceremony was conducted under rigid rules of etiquette, with all speeches and replies written out and agreed beforehand. I always find it amusing to hear a Brit complain about the 'absurdities which seem to be the natural product of a culture and etiquette based on slavish adherence to Chinese precedents' when the British monarchy and parliamentary system are tied up in the most ridiculous and embarrassing rituals that, to this day, leave anything the Japanese have mustered far behind. Brunton, being a good Victorian, sees no hypocrisy in his criticisms.

Brunton was introduced by Itō Hirobumi. The Meiji Emperor thanked Brunton for his work and urged him to keep hard at it. Ushered out soon after, Brunton then attended a banquet in his honour at which 'all differences were sunk and congratulations exchanged', which I read as a euphemistic way of saying 'we all got shitfaced'.

By the start of 1872 it was time for Brunton to have a break. Fourteen lighthouses, two lightships, twelve buoys and three beacons were in service. The Brunton family had left Britain almost four years earlier and despite half of Eliza's siblings being in Japan, the urge to see family and sink into the comfort of home was strong. On 24 April 1872 the four Bruntons left Yokohama on the *Phase*, arriving in London on 18 June.

Brunton, obviously, didn't really do holidays, and his account of this period deals solely with Iwakura Mission, a two-year round the world diplomatic and fact-finding embassy. In charge was Foreign Minister Iwakura Tomomi (hence the Iwakura Mission), along with government ministers Kido, Itō, Okubo, and Yamaguchi, and an army of clerks, commissioners, officials and students, totalling 108 people in all, including five girls. The average age was thirty-two. This wasn't a government jolly; it was a serious research project aimed at catalysing the next stage of modernisation. It was also a diplomatic push to renegotiate the Unequal Treaties which were up for revision on 1 July 1872.

Among the group was Kume Kunitake, who kept the official diary, published in English in an abridged form as *Japan Rising*. I once spent a delightful week in the National Library of Scotland, Edinburgh, poring over the five unabridged volumes of the diaries.

Heading always west, they left Japan on 23 December 1871 and landed in San Francisco on 16 January 1872. Three of the five girls, Yamakawa (eleven), Nagai (ten) and Tsuda (six) were left behind in San Francisco to receive an American education, returning to Japan in 1882 (the other two girls, both fourteen, fell ill and returned to Japan after a few months). Janice P Nimura's excellent book *Daughters of the Samurai* tells their fascinating and difficult story much better than I could in this short space. The rest of the group took the train down through California, across the US, hitting Nevada, Utah and Chicago, before arriving at the east coast. On 6 August they left Boston by steamer and arrived in Liverpool on 16 August. They then split into two groups, one going south to London, the other going north.

It was here that Brunton met up with them. He makes no comment about his family who, presumably, were packed off to the in-laws, but he heads straight for the embassy where Parkes is also in attendance and joins the mission. I can't help but think this timing for his trip home wasn't a coincidence – the mission would have been a long time in planning, and Brunton must have known all about it through Parkes, Itō, and the others he knew. One can't help but wonder if this was his plan all along.

Brunton writes that Itō and his retinue attached themselves to him and he took them on a tour of businesses all over the city including, but not limited to 'the making of candles...glue... bricks...watches and clocks, pottery and terra-cotta, gunpowder...

tanning, dyeing and bleaching, meat-preserving'. Everything was studied, interrogated, recorded. The idea was to gather as much information as they could about modern industrial capitalism and so in time do away with the need for people like Brunton. In a sense, he was aiding them in his own obsolescence.

From London they travelled to Birmingham and visited factories making weapons, glass, chemicals, pens. Then came Liverpool and Manchester. Across the border they saw mining and shipbuilding on Clydeside, banking in Edinburgh, where the entire mission was reunited. In Edinburgh Brunton took them to see the Bell Rock Lighthouse, no doubt drawing attention to its longevity and his own work at Mikomotoshima, although the weather in October wasn't ideal for a day trip into the North Sea. Continuing through the Highlands and then back down to Newcastle and Yorkshire, they finally arrived back in London. Brunton was put to work fulfilling errands for the Japanese guests until their departure for Paris on 14 December.

The Brunton family left Britain on 12 February 1873, landing on 4 April, nearly a year after they left.

It's a constant frustration that Brunton makes no reference to his living arrangements, to his wife, Eliza, and his sister-in-law, Mary. His daughter, also Mary, was a baby when they left Southampton, so the stress for Eliza of being a new mother in a far-off land must have been high. She had her second child in Yokohama without the benefit of much of a support network or clean running water. How did she feel? Was she adventurous or was this just part of a Victorian woman's lot? What were they doing all this time? The problems of history: our concerns today were not their concerns back then. Brunton perhaps could never have foreseen that his living conditions, daily routine and leisure time could be of interest 150 years later, so made no mention of them. The Yokohama Archives book reproduces a photograph of Eliza from 1868. It's a studio photograph in which she stands, formally, somewhat uncomfortably, leaning on a waist-high table, her hands folded demurely on its surface, a dramatic curtain in the background. She is wearing a neck-to-floor dress, all properly Victorian buttoned up and not an inch of ankle. In the sepia print it's impossible to make out the colour but it seems striped and has a big bustle. Her long hair is tightly pinned into a stylish pleat giving her a slightly severe look, but her face is young, beautiful, strong, perhaps a touch playful. She may have been adventurous; she must have been strong. It's easy to read too much into a single photograph when that's all there is.

Brunton does, however, take a chapter in his memoir to deal with the issue of 'Women's Education in Japan'. While in Britain the embassy prompted Brunton to hire three women to 'teach Japanese women household duties as known and practised in Great Britain' at a school for women in Tōkyō. To this end he enlisted a matron, a governess and a seamstress. Brunton explains that he was hesitant to complete this task knowing that Japan was, at the time, a strongly patriarchal society and that Itō had made it clear they were to provide 'a merely mechanical education' not to 'alter the recognised position of their [the Japanese] women'. He and Parkes exchange letters on the subject and while Brunton must be praised for recognising the oppressed state of women in Japan at the time, the epistles are also beacons of classism, racism and misogyny as practised in the Victorian 'West'. They worry about sending 'a person of superior feeling and refinement' to a 'society, the moral and ethical standards of which were so completely opposed to those of Europe'. Parkes even gets a dig in about the negative repercussions should they hire American over European women. In the end, these three women are hired and travel to Japan with the Bruntons, no doubt gaining much insight from Eliza en route. Brunton tells us that though the school ran for a while, the experiment was not a success and wasn't repeated.

The Iwakura Mission continued through France, Belgium, the Netherlands, Prussia (as it then was), western Russia, Denmark, Sweden, Italy, Austria, Switzerland, France (again), Spain and Portugal before sailing through the Suez Canal and home via Sri Lanka (then called Ceylon), Hong Kong and Shanghai. They arrived home on 13 September 1873.

As Brunton points out, their mission was in one sense a failure: the renegotiation of the treaties was rejected by the Treaty Powers.

The Unequal Treaties would remain in place until 1899. Brunton attributes to this failure a downturn in good feeling between foreigners and the Japanese. The failure

> seemed to them not only a slur on their civilisation but also a humiliating personal stigma. Little wonder, therefore, that their association with foreigners became strained, their dealings with them less frequent, and their readiness to be influenced by them almost destroyed.

Brunton displays a rare burst of empathy here, showing that despite all his complaining, Japan and the Japanese had won him over. He considers Itō to be a friend and wants his plans to come to fruition. The mood is quickly broken as he goes on to enumerate how this new cold attitude frustrated him personally, taking his rage out on 'functionaries' over chapters like 'The Japanese in Bad Temper', 'Maintaining Discipline' and 'Keeping up the Standard'.

The failure of the Iwakura Mission to renegotiate in conjunction with the newfound military confidence brought about by the Taiwan expedition goes some way to explaining the more militant direction the Meiji government would take over the next few decades. It also goes some way towards explaining why Brunton and many of the other yatoi's days were numbered.

21. *Irōzaki Lighthouse*

Shimoda is, in a sense, where this whole story started. While Yokohama became the settlement, it was Shimoda that first felt the presence of the Americans. When Commodore Perry returned, as threatened, in 1854, negotiations took place at Ryōsenji Temple. Gyokusenji Temple was handed over first as a residence for Perry and his officers, and then as the home of the US Consulate in Japan, run by Consul General Townsend Harris. Near Ryōsenji today is a museum to this history. The temple's graveyard contains the remains of US sailors from Perry's fleet. There is also a plaque marking the spot where the first cow was killed for food on Japanese soil. It's hard to believe, given the love of beef and the pride the nation takes in native Wagyu brands such as Kōbe-gyu and Hida-gyu, that it has only been on the menu for a few generations, and it all started with a single slaughter in Shimoda.

There's an apocryphal story that I will indulge in for a tangential moment. Russian sailors, it goes, were shipwrecked off the coast of Hokkaido sometime during the Sakoku period. They were rescued and looked after while they waited to be repatriated. Some of their cargo was washed ashore as well, including a crate or two of red wine. The Hokkaido locals, never having encountered wine, reported back to their leaders than these outsiders drank blood by the bottle.

At Shimoda two lighthouses remain, Irōzaki and Mikomoto-shima. Irōzaki is on the mainland and should present no significant problems other than distance from home. Shimoda will have to be an overnight trip. Perhaps a couple of nights. Maybe I can loop in Tsurugisaki in Kanagawa while I'm at it and knock off all the remaining eastern lighthouses in one go, bar Kinkasan, of course, which may prove to be my bête noire. The other, Mikomotoshima, is going to be a bit of a problem.

Balanced on a tiny island 11 km offshore, there seems no way of getting there other than chartering a boat, befriending someone in the Coastguard or doing something stupid with a canoe. I put it on the backburner and focus on Irōzaki for the moment. There's going to come a time when either I put my hand deep in my pocket or admit that for the moment not every lighthouse is attainable. It may not matter. I'm not Dave Gorman after all, and I didn't bet anyone.

Mikomotoshima was Brunton's first lighthouse in Japan, one of the most pressing given its location, and perhaps the most difficult. Mikomotoshima is only technically an island. Really, it's a big rock jutting above the waves, the kind that has devastated shipping for millennia.

Around the time we went to Tomogashima, Minori called me into the living room where she was watching some Japanese TV show. Tamori, a comedian and celebrity, was presenting a travel show where he visited weird places around the country. That week it was Mikomotoshima. As his boat rode the waves he explained to the camera how it had taken more than a year of paperwork and negotiations with the Coastguard, the Navy, and the government to get permission to visit the island. More than a year. This is a guy of the stature with a major TV network behind him. Great.

In the spring of 2021, I'd long-planned a massive road trip with Jason. We'd take the ferry from Osaka to Kagoshima and drive back the length of Kyūshū and through Yamaguchi bagging as many as eight of my remaining lighthouses. Jason didn't care too much about the lighthouses (few, I've discovered, do) but he's always up for adventure and, as spring approached it became even more pressing: Jason's wife Haruna had fallen pregnant. This would essentially be Jason's last chance at a multi-day road trip for many, many years.

There was only one problem: Covid. The tide was high, to paraphrase Blondie, and vaccines were months away. We weren't locked down, but fun was frowned on. By driving and camping we could limit our interaction with others – again, the joy of a travel project that takes you to far-flung isolated places – but that in itself presented a problem. Japanese number plates contain the name of the city or prefecture in which the car is registered. Not a code that geeks and dealers memorise, but the actual name written in actual kanji. This had created an unexpected boon in the field of harassment as out-of-town cars were seen as Covid spreaders. Tōkyō-area plates in particular were targeted, with a number of municipalities publicly announcing 'Don't you be coming round here with your big city ways, coughing all over us'. Minori and I saw a car in Gifu with Kawasaki plates sporting a sticker which said, in Japanese and English, 'I live here!' Taking a car with Gifu plates across half the country was dodgy. Jason was relaxed about it though.

'The kind of people who are going to harass us over having Gifu plates are the kind of people who are going to harass us about being foreign anyway, so fuck them.' Which was fair.

In the end, it got too risky, problems mounted, dates became tight. Our two-week road trip shrank to two nights, and the entire west of Japan was replaced with Shimoda. At the start of March we piled into my new yellow Suzuki Hustler, two burly guys in a tiny car, got the tunes on (The Delgados) and barrelled down the highway.

In many ways Jason is like the brother I never had. Despite him growing up in a Mormon family in Colorado, we share a remarkably similar outlook on life, and we share many overlapping experiences, including formative years working in cinemas, a love of rural Gifu, and ongoing weight/body image problems. We swap cinema anecdotes as I drive, argue about Coen Brothers and Kevin Smith movies, discuss kanji-studying apps, and dream-plan for future trips. Jason has been to forty-five out of forty-seven prefectures, missing out on only Aomori and Okinawa. I'm on forty-one. I'm sceptical about future trips: I've lost many friends to children. Like those who have left Japan, I hope to see them again someday.

'When *Terminator 2* came out, did people know Arnie was the good guy?' he says.

'I don't know. Because Cameron gives the game away early on. When he goes into the bar, playing it for laughs, using "Bad to the Bone" as the soundtrack. If you're paying attention, the reveal shouldn't be a surprise.'

'Yeah, but I mean with the promotion, the trailers.'

'I've no idea. I think I was eleven when it came out. I certainly didn't see it in the cinema.'

'No, me neither. Hang on.'

He Googles it while I wait for a truck to get back into the lane he left for no discernible reason.

'Yeah, here we go. It was revealed in the trailer. Totally ruined it in advance.'

'I was working in the cinema when *The Phantom Menace* came out,' I say.

'Me too.'

'They kept such a tight lid on the plot, the trailers just had flashes, moments out of context...'

'Lots of podracers.'

'Yeah. And then about two weeks before the release we got the merch in, including the soundtrack CD which had a track called "Qui Gon's Funeral".'

'I was also working in the cinemas when that movie came out. We were legit on opposite sides of the planet doing the same shit. However, we got our print three days late.'

'Fuck!'

'It was nonsense. Those days were great though, building the films from reels onto Christie platter systems. Man, at the risk of sounding like a geezer, the movie theatre kids now just plug in the hard drive and push a button. No fun.'

'We weren't allowed anywhere near the projectors. The projectionists were these grumpy mysterious guys wreathed in smoke who mentioned the union every two minutes. They were great guys though. We got the *South Park* print three weeks early and had a big watching party. Booze, snacks we liberated, a few tokes by the bins beforehand. That was a great job.'

'I remember watching that film from the projection booth that summer. I don't think I ever watched it beginning to end, but I was up there watching it and a hot woman named Meagan who worked at the ticket counter would come up to the booth for encounters that HR never heard about. That was a good year.'

'I never had any encounters.'

'I had a few but also had weird religious hang-ups that ruined most of them.'

'All my hang-ups were non-religious. I remember asking one woman who worked there out for a date and was so sure she'd say no that I literally hadn't thought through what to say next. When she said yes, I just kind of stood there in silence for a while.'

'Oh man, so much of that too, though. This girl wants to get with me? Clearly something is terribly wrong with her. I'm out.'

'That train of thought and I are old friends.'

We reach Shimoda at lunchtime, too early to check into our beachside cabin, so we head straight for the nearer of the two temples, Ryōsenji. Shimoda is a gorgeous small town built around a narrow inlet and river. We climb a hill to see the ruins of Shimoda Castle and from the top you can see the evolution of the settlement spelt out in the geography. Any nomadic people happening across this sheltered cove would immediately recognise its utility. It is perfectly suited for productive human habitation: deep, safe, convenient, protected yet open fertile land, fertile waters.

The town is well aware of its tourist value, with a memorial marking the exact spot where Perry set foot on Japanese soil (really? The *exact* spot?), and numerous cafés and souvenir shops. The streets are well tended, highlighting the old waterways, stone bridges and period buildings without fetishising them, as some towns do, and without smothering them in the cheapest, gaudiest veneer. This is a tourist destination and a living town. Ryōsenji is both a historical site and a working temple.

The Black Ships Museum is very well done, with English signage that is comprehensive, useful and clearly checked by a fluent English speaker - all rarities in Japanese museumdom. I'm impressed by Shimoda and kind of wish we were staying in the town rather than out at the beach - the nightlife looks like it could be fun.

We drive round to Gyokusenji which I've been wanting to see ever since I read about the plaque to the slaughtered cow. It's difficult to find, and we drive by the turning a couple of times before seeing it. The shrine itself is under renovation and there's little to see. After the excellent presentation of Ryōsenji it's a bit disappointing, but maybe we're just getting tired. We grab some lunch and drive to the beach. It's still too early to check in but we lie on the sand, drifting.

The beach looks directly out at Mikomotoshima which appears a lot closer than it had in my imagination. One thing I'm learning from this project is that I really am bad at visualising distances. It seems a lot more reachable from here, and so my spirits rise.

It's hard to describe the place where we're staying: built into the side of a cliff, it's ostensibly self-catering units but has the appearance of an Airbnb run by the Lost Boys (Peter Pan, not vampires). Entirely made of wood, sprawling across multiple levels, it is empty apart from two couples, and they sensibly put us at opposite ends of the complex. Each apartment has its own BBQ on the balcony, and there's a woodfire pizza oven anyone can use. This place could not be better designed for Jason and me. We do a supermarket run, stock up on everything we need to make a pizza, meat for the BBQ, and booze. Then it's taps aff, books out, wine open and lazing in the sun for the rest of the day.

Irōzaki turns out to have been a slight wild goose chase. One of the first lighthouses built by Brunton, it was finished in October 1871 and then destroyed in 1932 by a storm. This lighthouse dates from 1933, rebuilt to his design. Still, it's a beautiful location, high on the cliffs overlooking a vibrant Pacific. We follow the path out beyond the lighthouse to a shrine literally on the rocks. It's encased in a wooden shed, and through the floorboards the waves batter the cliffs. Birds of prey circle overhead, diving into the scrubs, resurfacing. The whole area is a geopark and signs dot the landscape explaining the geology, the flora and fauna. It's heaven to a nerd like me. This is end of the world stuff, another movie location.

Disappointed but happy, we return to our accommodation and mix up the dough for pizza bases, cracking the wine early. While it's setting, we hike along the cliff line. A bay away there's a cave network that looks enticing, but the wine and the beach entice more. Trips with friends means finding that Venn diagram of preferences, and Jason and I have found ours: enough sightseeing to justify relaxing. We have the pizza oven to ourselves, and there's a guitar free for all, so that's us set for the evening. I may not have actually got an original Brunton lighthouse done but I've had a great trip with a good friend, probably the last for the foreseeable future.

I load the car while Jason checks out. A woman is milling around the car park, like she's not sure whether she wants to speak to me or not. Finally, she decides, and comes over brandishing two peaches as a gift.

'You're from Gifu?' she asks in English.

'Yes,' I say. 'You're local?'

'I'm from Hiroshima originally. This is my business.'

'Oh, you're the owner? It's wonderful here, we had a great stay.'

'Thank you. My son runs it now. How did you find us?'

'Just online.'

'I hope you had a good trip. Did you visit anywhere?'

'We looked around Shimoda and went up to Irōzaki Lighthouse.'

'Oh, have you been out to Mikomotoshima? That lighthouse was built by a British man, Brunton.'

'I know Brunton! He's from near my hometown. But I didn't think you could visit Mikomotoshima. I really want to!'

'People kayak out, if you're fit enough. Or I could ask one of my fishermen friends to take you out.'

'Ah! I wish I'd known earlier. We have to go back today.'

'Next time, mention it when you're booking, we can help organise it.'

'I will. I'll be back soon!'

22. The Final Years

Given corporate Japan's attitude towards time off (you can get a few days in May, a couple in August, and a handful at New Year, and that's only out of the goodness of your boss's heart), it's hard to imagine how they would react today to someone taking a year off to go home. Reading between the lines, and given what was to happen next, perhaps they were quite happy to have Brunton out of their hair for eleven-and-a-half months. It's hard not to look at the timeline and Brunton's memoir and not conclude that his holiday showed the authorities that, despite his protestations to the contrary, Brunton wasn't irreplaceable.

The Bruntons arrived back in Yokohama on 5 April 1873 after nearly two months at sea. While he'd been away, work had continued. Ground was broken on Nosappu, on the east coast of Hokkaido, and Omaezaki, Shizuoka. Tomogashima in Wakayama and Anorisaki in Mie were lit for the first time, and Wadamisaki at Kobe and Tenpōzan in Osaka moved from temporary to permanent lights. A number of buoys and other lights went up too. In short, everything continued on course, testament to the efficient and organised system he'd put in place but laying the ground for his own eventual obsolescence.

He got straight back to work touring sites and planning for the future. In August 1873 he was asked to put together plans for developing Yokohama Harbour. Yokohama had been chosen by the government more for its distance from the Japanese population than for its suitability for international shipping. Nagasaki was more developed and there were high hopes for Kōbe and Ōsaka, but Yokohama was close to the capital, it was where the embassies were based, and therefore suitable or not, it was to be the main port. The fact that in 1873 it still didn't have a proper pier or wharf is more than a little surprising. Most cargo ships were unloaded by a small flotilla.

The scheme was to dominate much of Brunton's time over the next few years and grew to be 'one of considerable magnitude, embracing the construction of two-mile long piers enclosing five hundred acres of water, and estimated to cost $2,500,000' (roughly $85,000,000 in today's money). A small-scale plan drawn up by Brunton dating back to 1870 had never gone anywhere. By 4 September 1873, he had completed a second more elaborate plan that would accommodate at least eighteen ships. This was then expanded further in March 1874 and again in October 1874.

The Yokohama Archives book reports that at the same time, the Dutch engineer C J van Doorn, also employed by the Japanese government, had drawn up rival plans for a harbour. There were fundamental differences between the two approaches, not least for the foundations which Brunton wanted to be concrete while van Doorn wanted fascine (a bundle of wooden rods commonly used in military operations on wet ground). Needless to say, this wasn't a disagreement confined to paper.

On 18 March 1874 the Emperor himself travelled to Yokohama to inspect the lighthouse facility and to see the harbour plans for himself. He arrived 'on horseback, with a large retinue and accompanied by the Empress and her suite, in carriages all arrayed gorgeously in silk'. Somewhat down the pecking order, Brunton was eventually presented to the Emperor. Through an interpreter (Hayashi, who would go on to become ambassador to Britain), Brunton outlined his harbour plans with the help of a 3D model prepared for the occasion. Afterwards, the Emperor was given a guided tour of the establishment, dwelling particularly on the lamps themselves. Brunton writes that the Emperor 'expressed himself as much gratified'. After dinner, the *Japan Weekly Mail* reported on 21 March, the Emperor was led out onto the night-time balcony to see the full effect of the lamps in action. It's easy to imagine Brunton proudly showing off his achievements. The next day was an open day for the public to see what their Emperor had witnessed the day before. Thousands came, though one wonders how many would have bothered if the Emperor hadn't led by example.

In May 1874 the Finance Ministry presented plans to Sanjo

Sanetomi, the grand minister of state, 'without specifying which construction method or expenditures would be involved'. The Emperor's enthusiasm clearly wasn't contagious; Sanjo kicked the proposals down the road. The Finance Minister tried again later with Brunton's March 1874 plans but got no further. Brunton produced a more detailed price estimate in January 1875 but the project was doomed during Brunton's time in Japan. The harbour, following Brunton's plans, was finally built between 1889 and 1896, when it was also connected to the burgeoning rail network.

At the same time, the faithful *Thabor* was in urgent need of a refit. Everything necessary for the job existed at the Yokosuka dockyard, built by the French and opened in 1871. Brunton began the process of the refit in April 1872, just prior to leaving for home, but he held little hope in the French artisans and their Japanese workers doing the job in the kind of timely manner he usually demanded. Sure enough, by August 1873, during which time Brunton had been abroad for a year and returned, work still hadn't begun, new boilers having been ordered from France. Brunton 'offered to obtain competent men' but was rebuffed. By February 1874, 'some progress had been made'. By May 28, 'no date for the completion of repairs' could be given. On 6 July 1874 the boilers were finally installed but the decks had yet to be laid. Brunton finally snapped, took back the ship and had it refitted under his own command using Chinese workers. The work was done in a few weeks. Brunton laid the blame at the feet of the Japanese workers though given Brunton's previous encounters with his French engineering peers, I think it highly likely that this was a simple act of petty sabotage. If you spend four years insulting someone, belittling their work, and using your political contacts to grab jobs from under their noses, you can't really expect them to do you a favour when you need it.

Now the ship was back in service he took an inspection tour around Japan, leaving on 2 August and returning 3 October 1874. Parkes notes in a letter that Brunton had to return without inspecting all the lighthouses but no information is given as to why. Rather Parkes seems to share Brunton's concern that work is being done on some of the iron lighthouses without his involvement.

Upon his return, Brunton learned that his Japanese superiors had ordered a replacement for the aging *Thabor* to be built by Robert Napier & Sons, shipbuilders, in Glasgow. Predictably outraged, he takes great delight in detailing how Parkes refused to set foot on the vessel despite numerous invitations. It is with amusement that he notes it was later sold to a private merchant and ran aground.

As previously mentioned, in 1874 Brunton notes a change in attitudes towards foreigners in general and those in direct employment in particular. Brunton takes umbrage at this, interpreting it as a personal slight and places the cause firmly in bruised official ego. The plan always was for the yatoi to train their own replacements, the entire scheme relying on built-in obsolescence, but Brunton's view of the Japanese, both workers and officials, clearly leads him to conclude that in his case this could never happen. He complains of European workers being sidelined 'into positions of mere drudges without authority or influence', a sentiment which anyone who worked for a Japanese language school can sympathise with, but which as I have said, was the plan all along.

Beauchamp, in his notes to his edition of Brunton's memoir, points out that there was actually a power struggle going on in the government between 'old conservatives and the progressives for control of the future direction of policy' while Cortazzi explains that the government was buffeted by a financial crisis. In addition, as we have already seen, the failure of the Iwakura Mission to renegotiate the Unequal Treaties created a certain amount of ill-will. Brunton was merely caught in the crossfire of this political and economic storm, though his egocentric view of things ensured that he concluded every government action was directed at him personally. These political and economic storms, detailed more clearly in *The Meiji Restoration* by W G Beasley, would go some way to explain why the harbour plan never got off the ground. A foreigner suggesting they spend two-and-a-half million dollars at this time was unlikely to make much headway, regardless of the soundness of the scheme.

Brunton wouldn't take any of this lying down. His constant undercurrent of frustration is no longer cut with wry humour. His memoir from this point on becomes a litany of complaints, some justified, many petty. He characterises his time from 1874 onwards as 'one long continued struggle, maintained with varying success on either side'. He credits Itō Hirobumi, at that time head of the Public Works Department, with ensuring that the vital work of lighthouse construction proceeded, but with many grudging compromises from Brunton.

Clearly aware of which way the wind was blowing, a 'voluminous book of instructions' is compiled and translated detailing the roles and duties of lighthouse keepers though Brunton despairs at the quality of men entrusted with this job. He is rightly proud of reports from incoming ships about the quality of his lights but, like all highly controlling men, assumes everything will fall apart the second he turns his back.

The surest sign of his contract coming to an end is when Eliza and the children leave Japan on 15 December 1874. Brunton never mentions his family, and the Archives only note that she left, leaving the record frustratingly blank. Cortazzi simply notes that she left on the 'British steamer *Bombay* bound for Hong Kong'.

Around this time, plans for the Imperial College of Engineering were underway. The ball was rolling as early as 1872 and while the Iwakura Mission was in Britain, Itō signed off on the hiring of Brunton's nemesis Henry Dyer. This perhaps explains why Brunton never mentions the school in his manuscript. Cortazzi, by contrast, in the appendices reproduces a series of letters in the *Japan Weekly Mail* from 1875 that are, frankly, hilarious. Yokohama Archives of History have the full series of newspapers and it reads like nothing so much as a Twitter spat between two Victorian white men who believe they are infallible. There's no way Dyer and Brunton didn't know each other personally and one can only assume these two Scots, east and west coast with all the assumptions of each other that contains, conducted their war of words amongst the social milieu of Yokohama and Tōkyō. Brunton, it has to be said, comes off worse. While his points about practical training, arising no doubt from his experience of working with Japanese labourers, may have merit, like all angry white men on social media, his high-handed tone, general air of superiority, and barely concealed insults undermine any point he was trying to make. Dyer comes across as more balanced, more rational, and far less petty. It's hard not to interpret Brunton's attacks on Dyer in light of him having been overlooked (in his view) for the position.

The context for these letters, and at least part of the explanation for his belligerent public attitude, is that in March 1875 Brunton was given a one-year notice of the termination of his contract. Itō calls him to Tōkyō and meets with him personally and promises to find him employment elsewhere in Japan (perhaps his mind immediately turned to the college?) but within three days news filtered through that there was nothing to be done, and that Brunton's work was finished. He concludes that Itō didn't have the authority to offer Brunton new employment, and Itō's letter of thanks, which Brunton reproduces, is certainly fulsome and flowing with praise. Conversely, it's easy to see a retinue of Japanese officials, mocked, browbeaten and enraged by Brunton's behaviour and attitude over the previous seven years, only too happy to see the back of him. If the spat with Dyer was some kind of public application for a job at the college it completely failed.

On 12 November 1875 Brunton set off on his last tour of Japan. Parkes joined him on the *Thabor* as they circled the coastline landing at every lighthouse built to that date. Overall, they are satisfied though Brunton's perfectionist bent can't help noticing avoidable 'defects'. Arriving at Kagoshima to inspect Satamisaki on 9 December, Parkes suggests they continue on to the 'Riu Kiu Islands'. They arrive in Naha two days later.

The history of Okinawa is fascinating. Originally an independent kingdom, Ryūkyū had long been claimed by Japan and China. Akamine Mamoru's excellent book *The Ryukyu Kingdom: Cornerstone of East Asia* shows how, for centuries, Ryūkyū kings played the two powers off against each other, ensuring their own freedom and prosperity. This lasted as long as Japan and China were relatively equally matched. As soon as China started to wane, Japan seized the opportunity, declaring Okinawa a prefecture in 1879. China still nominally lays claim to it today but while there are roughly 29,000 US troops stationed there, no one's really rocking the boat.

Brunton departs from his usual style here and adopts the tone of a naturalist or sociologist. He's still the same Victorian patriarch looking down on these primitive islanders, but you can tell from his chapter on the islands and his paper 'Notes Taken During a Visit to Okinawa Shima - LooChoo Islands', which he presented to the Asiatic Society of Japan on 19 January 1876 and which was then printed in the *Japan Weekly Mail* three days later, that the spirit of adventure and exploration is upon him. At this point he knows his job is over and is perhaps in something akin to a holiday humour. I know from my own experience that trips back to Scotland from Japan, while welcome, don't really feel like holidays, not in the way that going somewhere new and exotic does. Parkes and Brunton returned to Yokohama in the new year.

One of Brunton's last acts in Japan was to draw up a complete 1:1,250,000 (20 miles to 1 inch) scale map of the country. At this point perhaps no one had travelled more extensively around Japan, though the majority of his travels were confined to the extremities. Drawing on Satow's earlier scholarship and using Japanese survey data (perhaps drawn up by McVean in his work at the Survey Department, another tantalising glimpse into the wider network of Yokohama life), he put together the most comprehensive map of Japan ever produced using the British Ordnance Maps as a model. It was this map that Isabella Bird relied on when she arrived in Japan two years later.

23. *Tsunoshima Lighthouse*

Because of the pandemic, for nearly two years I didn't leave home. The universities were teaching remotely and, as Minori is a nurse, we were isolating pretty hard. We got the same itchy feet as everyone, desperate for the day it became okay to visit the in-laws, go to a restaurant, go camping for a night. I'd planned to be finished this trip, finished this book, by 2020 but I couldn't even leave my village let alone tour the country visiting lighthouses. Those two nights in Minami-Izu with Jason had been grabbed in between 'states of emergency' but I still had eleven lighthouses to go. Covid or not, I needed to get back out on the road.

In January 2022 the Japanese government introduced a 'quasi state of emergency' which has all the rhetorical weight of your dodgy uncle saying 'Don't do anything I wouldn't do' before you head off to a party. It was the beginning of a long, painfully slow de-escalation. It was good enough for me. I started planning my trip to Yamaguchi, Kyūshū and Shikoku to knock off eight of them.

In the days leading up to departure I started feeling increasingly stressed about the whole thing. I couldn't pinpoint why at first: I'd driven around Japan loads of times before. I'd travelled alone countless times. As I pondered, I came to the understanding that I'd become, in a small way, institutionalised. Something of a shut in. I'd grown so used to being at home that the thought of not being at home was slightly terrifying. In two years of Covid I'd gone from being desperate to be on the move to plausibly road-shy. That was not right. Not on. I had to get out as soon as possible. Yet the night before departure I had anxiety dreams about car crashes, about heart attacks and strokes, about earthquakes and tsunamis. I said goodbye to my wife like I'd be away for years. This new normal was much like Nu Metal – not something I could live with.

Once I was on the road I felt better. I drove 500 km and spent the night in Fukuyama, having an early dinner before everything closed and walking around the castle grounds – the castle itself was wrapped in scaffolding and tarps undergoing renovations for its 400th anniversary. Another problem with travelling during Covid was that every tourist site in Japan had taken the opportunity to close for refurbishment. Sensible, but a tad annoying.

The next morning, I was back on the road, steaming down the highway in Woodstock. I always feel bad taking the highway, the voice of Robert M Pirsig, author of *Zen and the Art of Motorcycle Maintenance,* in my ear, explaining how highways bypass real life, lift you up and over all the things you're travelling to see. Highways are about reaching the destination as fast as possible; roads are about the journey. However, it's going to take me two weeks to see eight lighthouses and that's using the highways. Regular roads would add another week or so. I would drive more than 1,000 km to see Tsunoshima alone. So sorry, Pirsig, but I'm taking the highway.

Between Fukuyama and Hiroshima, the landscape is mountainous and the Sanyo Expressway climbs with it, affording the driver snatched glances across pine-covered peaks. This morning it's misty, the sun rising over a cold land, giving the mountains that samurai movie feel. Between the steep slopes old Japan remained, the terraced rice fields, fruit trees, rows of tea bushes, the odd farmhouse, or small compound of houses as generations spread into their own space. Perhaps if I were off the highway I could enjoy this more; maybe the reality would overwhelm the fleeting impression my imagination could work its magic on. For the moment, these bursts of cinematic Japan lift my spirits and make me grateful to be travelling once more.

This is my first time in Yamaguchi, not counting flashing through on the shinkansen (bullet train). My expectations aren't high. The only two things I know for sure about Yamaguchi is that there is a lot of industry and it shares its name with the largest crime family in Japan, the Yamaguchi-gumi. This is just a coincidence – the yakuza mob were started in Kobe by a guy called Yamaguchi – so the association is unfair, but as I know little else about the most westerly prefecture on Honshū, that's all that's in the bank when I make a Yamaguchi withdrawal. My unfair preconceptions aren't helped by first impressions: I come off the highway at Mine to a vista of smoke stacks, factories and associated metal monstrosities. A few miles further on I pass Mine Rehabilitation Centre, Japan's first private prison, opened to 'alleviate the problem of overcrowding in the penal institutions'. Sorry Yamaguchi, but so far I'm bang on the money.

Industry gives way to bland hills and featureless fields. After two days of highways, I'm stuck behind an old driver doing 30 km/h in a 50 zone (a daily hazard in an aging society) and trying not to get frustrated. As if to reinforce my first impressions, every five minutes I see another cop car. It would be ironic to be done for speeding now.

The slow pace does leave me time to notice differences. Architecture is divergent here, showing the influence of being much closer to the continent than Gifu. Temple roofs are simpler, smoother, more rounded than the sharp, inflected temples I'm used to. The roofs on houses are distinct too, with a preponderance of red tiles, a marked contrast to the black/grey and occasional blue I'm used to. Perhaps it's something to do with average temperatures, black holding the heat more and so is desirable in snowy Gifu but unwelcome in the sweltering south.

All of a sudden the scenery changes – I'm much higher up than I realised. To my left I look down into a valley. From this distance the fields are rich yellows and greens. A river snakes through them, homes radiating out to the hills which erupt suddenly from the flat valley floor. Ahead of me the Japan Sea, a tapestry of blues and whites. The sky is clear but there must be a wind out there, the white peaks visible from this far away. My mood is up, the Aberdonian in me cheered by the sight of the sea, the island of Tsunoshima ahead.

Tsunoshima is joined to the mainland by a big bridge, imaginatively named Tsunoshima Ōhashi – Tsunoshima's Big Bridge. Brunton would have come by boat, long before this bridge was thought of, so he would have approached from the far side. South Korea – Busan to be specific – lies roughly 190 km across the water. This is the closest the mainland of both nations comes although there are plenty of islands between here and there, including Tsushima, claimed by both and the cause of much diplomatic dick swinging over the last few decades. I'd briefly considered looping Tsushima into this trip, planting a flag, claiming the island for Scotland just to be daft, get a good photo, but I'm doing enough daft things without causing an international incident as well. I take a few photos alongside a group of bikers before crossing.

Tsunoshima Lighthouse

The lighthouse is on the far side of Tsunoshima, looking out towards the continent. It's a proper tourist set up: three big car parks, roadside cafés and stands. Everything is closed apart from one car park and one café, both of which are half full despite the season and the pandemic. I guess lighthouses are a great pandemic destination – outside windy spots, lots of space, easy to feel safe and distanced.

There are about twenty people milling about but none are up the lighthouse so I have the place to myself. It's 30 m high, 45 m above sea level, and from the gallery you get a perfect panoramic view. This coastline is flat so Brunton couldn't borrow much height from the landscape. Nothing for it but to go straight up. Work began in August 1873 and it was lit on 1 March 1876.

The quarters are intact and have been turned into a museum, and nearby there is a gift shop that sells postcards, watercolours of lighthouses across Japan. I buy a set, partly for the memory, partly to support the artist, but mainly because I spend so long complaining about Japan's crappy gift shops that when I find one doing something even a little interesting, I have to put my money where my mouth is. The museum has photos of some lighthouses taken around the time of illumination and I snap the snaps, useless from a copyright point of view but perfect for comparing past to present, especially for the ones that have changed or been rebuilt.

After two days of little but driving I take great pleasure in strolling along the coast, kicking pebbles on the beach, sitting on benches looking out at Korea. There are certain aspects of old age I feel I can embrace wholeheartedly and one of them is the joy of sitting contemplatively in front of a bit of nature. There are surfers out and, as always, it looks fun but not my bag. I'm a watcher far more than a doer.

Hunger takes over and I drive back to the Michi-no-Eki (roadside service area with restaurants and shops) and partake of some curry-rice. The menu boasts kujira-curry-rice – whale curry – and the server recommends it, but I pass. There's a line where curiosity and principles meet and it is here. One last look at the lighthouse high above everything else and I drive on. Without the bridge, the island would be dead. The bridge and the lighthouse give people an excuse to come and the island has done a great job of capitalising, building things, especially for families. I feel refreshed, glad I pushed myself to leave the safety of home and the comfort of routine. That's one of eight for this trip bagged.

With an hour or so to kill until I check in to my Airbnb, I follow a road more twisted than a Dan Brown plot (more potholed too) to a little fishing village called Tsuno, which Google Maps tells me has a café called Bliss Point. I've learned to take everything Google Maps says with more than a pinch of salt and sure enough, I roll into a one-road town only just wide enough for my car to pass. If I'd encountered anyone else on the way, one of us would've ended up in the sea. The café turns out to be off-road, up some narrow stairs, round a corner, up some more stairs, past a rundown house, and into the garden of another house. I open the door to the house and call, but there is no answer. There are shoes, however, and a bottle of hand sanitiser. I shrug, take off my shoes and wander through to the living room. A woman sitting drinking coffee looks up, surprised, before calling out 'konnichiwa'. This brings another woman who, in heavily accented English, confirms I'm not in fact in someone's house.

'You found us on Google Maps, yes?'

'Yes.'

She laughs. 'Everyone who finds us on Google Maps has that confused expression. Welcome.'

I order lunch and once she's finished serving everyone else, she comes over to practise her English. We chat a bit and she shows me around. I mentioned the roofs, the colour and ask her why.

'No idea. But it's pretty.'

'Are you from around here.'

'No, I live in Shimonoseki. I drive here three times a week.'

'Shimonoseki? That's like…'

'Two and a half hours. It's worth it though.'

I have questions, but someone calls from the dining room.

'Do you have time? Can I tell you about this café?' she says.

'Sure.'

We return to the main part of the café, she gets the refills seen to and then settles down on the floor in front of me with a small photo book.

'Is Japanese okay?'

'Sure.'

She launches into a presentation, using the photo book as her visual aid, and talks me through the history of her and her café. She's done this many times before and the talk has a practised quality. It is memorised and told with little thought for the audience. I laugh inwardly, thinking about my students and their awful presentations, and wonder if it's really something passed on, an inheritance, something in the water. She tells me about her dream to always run a café but life getting in the way, a career as a teacher, a husband and children who took priority, her daughters finally away to university she found this abandoned house miles from home and renovated it with a group of friends, one of whom died of cancer along the way. I'm nodding and smiling, giving the correct ohs and ums, but the last part almost passes me by until I realise she's said cancer. My face is giving all the wrong responses, the delay of translation making me look insensitive. I rearrange my face but it's doubtful she noticed. She finishes with a flourish.

'Finished.'

I ask a few questions but now that she's told her story she's ready to move on to other things. I pay up and head for the beach cottage I've rented, checking in and spending the remaining hours of sunlight clambering among the rock pools and writing a poem:

in the rockpools of Nagato
i find myself as a child
still jumping rocks, uncovering crabs
bursting the bladderwrack underfoot
tempting waves crash against the shore
and the warmth of exertion prickles his face
shipwashed rope and polished boards
ring of Long John Silver and Robinson Crusoe
in turn i am thrilled by the exposed cliffs
sedimentary layers, vibrant veins, the flow of deep time
his delight at what the sea brings in matched
by my delight at what the sea wreaks
we both feel the heat of curiosity
and reunite for a brief half hour
in the rock pools of Nagato

I wake before it's light and set off for Shimonoseki, thinking of the café owner doing this drive as a commute. It's a beautiful view but everything becomes routine in the end.

24. *Mutsurejima, Shirasu and Hesaki Lighthouses*

Today I'm hoping to bag three lighthouses, or two and a half realistically. Hesaki, Mutsurejima and Shirasu. The latter is on an uninhabited rock with no access. I'd hoped to find a fisherman to take me out but so far nothing. I've never been to Shimonoseki, don't know anyone in the area, and a search for fishing charters turned up nothing promising. The best I could hope for was seeing it from Mutsurejima, the next island over. The ferry to Mutsurejima is at 10 am and misjudging the roads badly I arrive around eight. I get a coffee and stroll around town, but everything is closed and anyway, the port of any city is never the pretty bit.

I climb to a little shrine overlooking the harbour, home to some nautical deity no doubt, and ask for a blessing for the trip. Up here it's really windy and the sea swell is daunting. I return to the ferry terminal and ask a postman if it's safe enough for the ferry.

'This? It's nothing.'

I don't mind being patronised. In these situations, a local dismissing your fears is exactly what you want. I'd be much more worried if he'd shrugged and said 'should be fine. Said your prayers?'

There are a few ferries every day but however I time it, I'm going to have hours to kill. Two dozen of us pile on and take our seats inside – this is a commuter ferry, not a tourist one – and settle in to watch the TV. It's the 2022 Winter Olympics in Beijing and today Japan is facing South Korea in the women's curling. This is a grudge match and apparently Japan's curlers are something of a sensation. Listening to the build-up amidst repeats of the earlier rounds, I understand that in the previous Olympics they came close. The five women are all from the same part of Hokkaido – two of them are sisters. After their almost-success, they received an influx of tax money. Japan has a strange tax system whereby you can pay your taxes in advance as a rough estimate but nominate a city authority to receive the money. The idea is to balance out the movement of people from the countryside to the city. Apparently, lots of people did this for the area the curlers are from and as such they suddenly had the ability to train properly in nice new facilities and with nice new equipment. Hopes have been raised.

We land before anything can be slid, and I head off in the direction of the lighthouse. It's a little one and, to my untrained eye, on the wrong side of the island. This side, facing the mainland, must be pretty well lit up at night, as the harbour is here. The other side has nothing but allotments and fruit trees. I guess they knew what they were doing.

Like Tsunoshima, Mutsurejima is made of granite. This gives me a warm feeling as Aberdeen is the home of granite. Brunton must have liked that too, being a northern boy. Although this would be local granite, or maybe Chinese. My grandparents are buried in Aberdeenshire with granite headstones, but the granite there is Chinese too. The world we live in.

Everything here is overgrown, and it's not even clear if the light can be seen from the sea. It's low down, not much above sea level, unimpressive after the tower at Tsunoshima. The foundations of the keeper's cottage are still there, but everything else is bamboo and creepers. I jump the locked gate to do the traditional laying on of hands and pick up a pebble for my cairn. No one's around. In fact, it feels like I'm the only one on the island.

Construction on Mutsurejima began in late 1870 and the lamp was lit on 1 January 1872. According to a sign by the lighthouse, on 12 June 1897, the Meiji Emperor visited the lighthouse, the first official lighthouse visit by an Emperor in Japanese history. I wonder if he remembered the Scotsman with mutton-chop whiskers who was presented to him in November 1871, twenty-six years earlier.

I return to the road and climb the hill, passing nothing but allotments and a radar station. The allotments are carved out of bamboo groves giving them the impression of hidden worlds. I guess it makes sense with the wind and salt to protect your crops as much as possible. From the highest point I can see over to Shirasu Island.

Mutsurejima Lighthouse

Despite my best efforts this is as close as I'll get to that lighthouse, 6 km, give or take. Ground was broken on Shirasu in early 1872 and lit temporarily on 1 December that year. The permanent light went up on 1 September 1873. The lighthouse is on the far side – the ocean side – of that uninhabited rock so I can't even see it. That's the best I can hope for though on this budget. I need a friendly helicopter owner. Two of today's three, three of the trip's eight are done and I'm enjoying this more than I expected.

I sit on the dock of the bay reading John Dougill's *In Search of Japan's Hidden Christians*, which is exactly my kind of thing: travel mixed with history as Dougill goes around Kyūshū visiting all the important sites related to this often-forgotten part of Japanese history. As I'm reading an old guy comes up and sits on the wall next to me.

'You here to see Miyagi-san?'

'No,' I say. 'I was visiting the lighthouse.'

'Not Miyagi-san?'

'No. Who is Miyagi-san?' Don't make a *Karate Kid* joke, Iain.

'I thought you were here to see Miyagi-san. Did you like the lighthouse?'

'Yeah, very nice. I'm writing a book-'

'You sure you're not here to see Miyagi-san?'

'Sorry. No. Should I see him? Is he famous?'

He's not one for answering questions. He nods and wanders off. I briefly think about trying to find this Miyagi-san but the ferry appears on the waves and I'm curious how the curling is going. Later I learn that Miyagi-san is leading something of a regeneration movement, bringing young people out to the island to prevent its eventual depopulation. Whenever a foreigner shows up, it's usually something to do with him.

I pick up the car and head south, crossing from Yamaguchi onto Kyūshū. The Kanmon Bridge is insanely high and long, more than a kilometre in length and 61 m above the water. The drive across must be amazing but being the driver, I can't enjoy it. My fear of heights means I can't take my eyes off the road for a second. I wonder what Brunton would make of it – the bridge in effect made some of this lighthouse work less necessary, since the majority of boats in this strait would have been crossing from Honshu to Kyūshū and back again – but more likely the engineer in him would be impressed.

I quickly reach Hesaki, another squat lighthouse (10 m) built high atop the thing. Constructed from December 1870, the Yokohama Archives have the illumination date as 1 March 1872, while the sign at the lighthouse says 22 January. It would be a nice spot for a picnic, especially as the daffodils are in full trumpet, but after the usual photos and stone gathering, I'm about done for the day. I put the foot down for Fukuoka and the refuge of two nights in the same place.

Hesaki Lighthouse

25. *Eboshijima Lighthouse*

The plan for the next day is a bit complicated. Even more so than Shirasu, Eboshijima Lighthouse is one of those I had asterisks next to from the start. It's on an uninhabited rock 16 km offshore. Like Mikomotoshima there are photos online of fishermen casting off from the rock but unlike Mikomotoshima I can't find any fishermen willing to take me there. The next best thing is the ferry to Ikishima and Tsushima, which passes it, I am reliably informed, 200-300 m offshore. That'll have to do. The vague idea of going to the disputed island of Tsushima and taking mildly provocative selfies is still festering at the back of my mischievous mind, and the excuse of riding the ferry there to see Eboshijima nearly pushes me over the edge.

Ikishima, on the other hand, is something of a domestic tourist spot, marketing itself as a tropical island à la Okinawa but much closer to home. White beaches, dolphins, water-worn caves, the works. It's also got an ancient history, including a stunning collection of Jōmon (14,000–3,000 BCE) burial mounds, the ruins of a sixteenth-century castle and areas connected with the Mongol invasion of the thirteenth century that gave rise to the original kamikaze – the wind of the gods, a typhoon that destroyed the Mongol hordes against this coastline. Not a bad way to spend a day.

Ancient history or current geopolitics? My decision is made by the timetables. I can do a round trip to Ikishima, leaving at eight and returning at six or I can stay overnight on Tsushima. Day trip it is. I sit up late with bus timetables making a plan to circumnavigate the island without getting stranded and missing the return ferry, when my weather app alerts me that a severe gale warning has been issued. Expect snow, big seas and high winds. In the morning I cross my fingers and go to the ferry terminal anyway. It doesn't seem all that bad for February.

'You can get there,' the woman at the ticket desk tells me, 'but we can't guarantee that you'll get back.'

I weigh up options. Apart from the extra expense, would a night on Ikishima be such a bad thing. I look out over the bay and see… nothing. Low cloud cover, and squalls off shore. The whole point was to get a good look at this lighthouse and now it seems like I might not be able to see it at all. Also getting back is kind of important. Minori is flying to Fukuoka tomorrow for a four-day jaunt around Kyūshū. As a nurse she gets precious little time off and I don't want to ruin the longest holiday she's had in a couple of years by being stuck on a different island. I give it up as a bad job.

Instead, I take the car along the coast, following various outcrops to see how close I can get while remaining on dry land. The weather clears while I'm standing on one of these cliff tops and I catch sight of the island, foreboding against the slate sea. So close. Tantalisingly close. But not tonight, Josephine.

The lighthouse stands high on top of Eboshijima. Work began in June 1873 and was completed on 1 August 1875. According to the tourism website the lighthouse was rebuilt in 1975 to strengthen it. I drive along to Kuratsu Castle and from there to Nagoya Castle, both dating from the late sixteenth century and Toyotomi Hideyoshi's invasion of Korea and China. Having conquered and united Japan, he needed something to do with an entire generation of samurai who knew nothing but fighting, and so sent them off to the mainland. In his *History of Japan* George Sansom tells of an incident where a foreign missionary, of the influx which started arriving in Japan around this time, unfurled a map of the world in front of Hideyoshi showing how small Japan was compared to China, introducing doubt to the great general for the first time.

Outside Kuratsu two old men sit on a bench drinking One Cup Sake in total defiance of Covid restrictions and the buffeting winds and snow flurries. One of them calls over to me in a gruff but friendly voice.

'You want some saké?'

'Thanks, but I'm driving. Are you not cold?'

'The saké warms us up. No work today?'

'No. I was trying to get to one of the islands but the weather…'

They both shrug, the look of men well used to the idiosyncrasies of the sea.

'I don't suppose either of you have a boat?'

'No. Used to. Just a small one for fishing.'

'Nothing beats fishing. Out on the water before dawn, saké and nibbles,' says his friend.

'Dried squid.' A look of beatific pleasure washes over them both.

'I'll leave you to it. Don't get too cold.'

'If you find a boat, let us know.'

'Will do.'

26. Iojima Lighthouse

Minori arrives and we putter around Sasebo, follow the coast down to Nagasaki visiting famous places associated with the hidden Christians. I feel torn about this. I've never been a fan of Christianity, having grown up in Scotland during the 1980s when sectarianism was rife (he says, as if it has disappeared). I was routinely put out of my RE class at school for disruptive behaviour, usually questioning the teacher who once explained our main focus should be on Christianity but that he was being forced to teach 'all that other foreign mumbo jumbo' to us. I made it my life's work to ruin this man's day whenever I had his class. In this, I was entirely successful.

Missionaries offend me. I don't care what you believe but anyone who thinks they have a right to travel the world telling people they should abandon their culture and be more like the missionary is just an arsehole in my book. I'm not saying the Japanese were right to torture and murder the hidden Christians or the missionaries, I'm just saying that history has shown they were right to keep this aspect of colonialism out of the country. Christianity brought with it white supremacy (this is what all those Trump supporters mean when they say 'Christian' – white) and Japan, as Chris Glenn writes, was dangerously flirting with this kind of infectious colonialism before the door was firmly bolted. Without that, who knows what Japanese culture would be like today.

Still, it makes for an interesting tourist trail, quite different from the usual Japanese sightseeing jaunts: churches, caves, crosses hidden in plain sight and statues of Mary disguised as Kannon.

While Minori is with me I put the lighthouses on hold, more or less. Iojima is out the south of Nagasaki, on one of many islands in the stream, but this one is connected to the mainland by a bridge. We start off in a traffic jam and by the end are alone, a common experience in lighthouse bagging. The lighthouse is white, newly painted, and in fact isn't the original. The dome is original, but

Brunton's tower was fatally damaged by the atomic bomb and was replaced in 1954. The current lighthouse stands hard against the foundations of the original, which act as a memorial to the fallen comrade. After not getting to see Eboshijima properly, it's nice to run my hands along the warm white walls. Construction on the original began mid-1869 and was lit temporarily on 14 July 1870, and permanently on 14 September 1871.

It's a beautiful clear day, with the calm sea glistening. The quarters have been converted into a museum, exactly the same as Tsunoshima, but it is closed. I peer through the windows at the usual photos, explanations. There is a shack with self-service coffee and tea, an honour system and a swing seat, we chill, swinging in the easy breeze, looking out over Nagasaki Bay, for a long time the only way in or out of Japan.

On Christmas Eve 1868 Brunton sailed into Nagasaki. He describes the city as 'one of the most beautiful, even as it is the safest in the world'. Nagasaki is a name that has long haunted imaginations, mine included, for exotic and morbid reasons. Beginning in 1633 the Tokugawa Shōgunate began introducing edicts that effectively isolated Japan from the outside world. The Sakoku period was ostensibly aimed at keeping foreign influence – particularly Christian missionaries – from subverting the rule of the Tokugawa family. There were a few instances where the membrane was breached either by dint of an accident such as a shipwreck or something more insidious like those pesky Jesuits, a story most movingly recounted in Endo Shusaku's *Silence*. One window remained open to the outside though, or perhaps more of a tradesman's entrance: Nagasaki.

The Dutch, being very modern and pragmatic about these things, put trade before religion and promised the Shōgunate there would be no Christ, Bibles or priests anywhere near the shores of Japan, something the Spanish and Portuguese resolutely refused to countenance. In return the Dutch were granted the right to live, land and trade from the tiny man-made island of Dejima off Nagasaki.

Built by digging a channel, filling it with water and covering it with a single well-guarded bridge, the Dutch took up residence in 1641 and remained until the Americans broke their monopoly with classic gunboat diplomacy. Goods such as silk, cotton and sugar came in on one side of the island and passed through into Japan, while porcelain, lacquerware and rice went the other way. Knowledge passed through this funnel as well, as is beautifully dramatised in David Mitchell's *The Thousand Autumns of Jacob de Zoet* where medical knowledge is jealously guarded but open to curious prising.

Dejima is still there today, though land reclamation in Nagasaki Bay has left it peculiarly far inland. The warehouses, factories and residences have been restored and the place is now a tourist attraction in a city that has much to offer tourists.

Two-hundred-plus years of proximity to foreign influence has had a significant effect on the character of Nagasaki. It is an open, friendly, cosmopolitan place. Once the country opened, the port retained its importance, becoming a trading hub not just for Europeans but also Russian and Chinese merchants, creating a melting pot that leaves traces today in the plethora of churches, names and local dishes.

For our purposes, one of the other main attractions is the home of Thomas Glover. Born in Fraserburgh in 1838, Glover was a man of ideas and energy who worked first for Jardine Matheson but quickly took to working for himself, establishing Messrs Glover, the name he was trading under when Brunton arrived in Nagasaki. Brunton doesn't mention meeting Glover directly but does mention his role in opening Takashima to coal mining. He visits the island and reports on its productivity before moving to discuss the lighthouse to be erected on Iojima in Nagasaki Bay.

I visited Dejima and Glover's house early in 2012. His house is very popular with tourists, being a rare example of British interior design on the archipelago, though my friends, Dan and Robert, found it strangely underwhelming, perhaps because of its familiarity. At one point, standing in the bedroom I remarked that my grandmother had once owned the exact same dresser, while Robert said the same about a chest of drawers. I've always found museums of the everyday to be lacklustre. A museum should contain the exotic, treasures from afar, ideally donated and not stolen in a fit of imperial kleptomania. They shouldn't contain my grandmother's dresser.

That 2012 trip to Nagasaki was memorable. Dan and Robert, old friends from Aberdeen University, arrived shortly after Christmas and stayed for a few weeks. We heeded the call of the Pet Shop Boys and went west calling at Hiroshima, Miyajima, Fukuoka (where we celebrated the New Year by carrying an inebriated Robert back to the hostel), Nagasaki, Beppu and Matsuyama before circling home.

Nagasaki once had a reputation both exotic and erotic, as the lyrics in that old jazz standard remind us:

Back in Nagasaki where the fellers chew tobaccy...
The way they entertain
Would hurry a hurricane...
They kissy and huggy nice
Oh, by jingo it's worth the price.

There was none of that on our trip, though Dan and I did leave Robert in a bar thinking we wouldn't see him until the next morning only for him to sheepishly knock on the door an hour or so later. No, Nagasaki's name no longer inspires images of smoky rooms and sultry women. Harry Truman saw to that.

Hiroshima and Nagasaki are forever bound together in the imagination. Kids in Britain, certainly when I was young, spent seeming decades studying World War Two. I'm sure there were other things on the curriculum but even they were tangentially related to the war. The rise of nationalism in Germany, the beginning of the welfare state. I'm sure if they could have crowbarred Churchill into the chemistry or home economics syllabus they would have. I must have been about eight when I first heard the words Hiroshima and Nagasaki. Atom bombs. August 1945. Mushroom cloud. I still have to pause before pronouncing Hiroshima, having learned the stress incorrectly at school. HiROshima. HIroshima. It was first, 6 August. Nagasaki met the same fate on 9 August. Pop quiz questions in primary school. Now I was standing in those cities. Ground zero.

Humans can make conflict out of anything. Out of nothing. There's something of a rivalry between Hiroshima and Nagasaki over remembrance. Hiroshima was first, primacy of the elder, the serious older brother worried about perception and face. Nagasaki, cosmopolitan, freer, more relaxed, making its own way, doing things its own way. The difference is striking when you visit both cities in quick succession.

The Hiroshima Peace Memorial Museum is, rightly, expectedly, a sombre, horrifying place. No punches are pulled. Here's what happened. Here's what they did. It gets the blood boiling, the fists clenching. The first time I went I nearly threw up. I was leafing through a book that contained photos taken in the immediate aftermath. Melted flesh. Skin hanging loose like a cowl. Crisp blackened bodies. Empty, shocked eyes. I had to sit. Breathe. It took a while to regain composure. On the way out a high school boy stopped me.

'You. American?'

'No.'

'Okay.' He walked away.

The museum does its job. You never forget. Nuclear = murder. I get it. However, the museum has taken a lot of criticism over the years, some of it fair. The bombing isn't presented in context. There is little mention of the rest of the war, a war that for Japan began in the early 1930s, perhaps the 1920s depending on how you view certain events, maybe during World War One if you count the seizure of German territory in China under British urging as an act of war (the Chinese do, and next time you're drinking Tsingtao beer, do a Wikipedia dive into the history of that brewery), possibly even as far back as 1910 if you include the annexation of Korea. No mention of any of it. The bombing is presented as a one-off, apparently random, act of madness. This in a country with a famously lacklustre approach to teaching the history of this period. I have, with my own ears, heard a junior high school student state that Pearl Harbour was a retaliation for the attack on Hiroshima, despite Pearl Harbour taking place four years before Hiroshima. Context is kind of important in a story like this.

Nagasaki by contrast takes a more objective, wider view. You get the war, the rise of militarism, the events and decisions on both sides that led to dropping the bombs, the other layers including the imminent involvement of the Soviet Union in the war, the message from Truman to Stalin to back off. To follow this for a second, this aspect of the bombing of Nagasaki is not just a side note: Stalin declared war on Japan on 8 August 1945. The day before Nagasaki was bombed, seven days before Japan surrendered. Opportunism on Stalin's behalf? Or an awareness of the Cold War to come? He saw the way it was going and wondered if he could get something out of it. He did, as I saw in Hokkaido.

Nagasaki Atomic Bomb Museum. Hiroshima Peace Memorial Museum. The difference in attitude is evident in the names. Nagasaki: we're going to confront this head on. Hiroshima: more indirect, euphemistic. Nagasaki gives context, starts earlier and goes later. The exhibition brings us up to date with nuclear testing and proliferation. Hiroshima is a wagging finger. Nagasaki is warning. Neither is right, neither is wrong, but two bombs, two cities, two vastly different reactions. Perhaps that eyehole of Dejima really did alter Nagasaki forever, giving the city a perspective the rest of enclosed Japan lacked.

We leave Nagasaki via the peaks of Unzen, where a huge volcanic eruption in 1991 killed forty-three people. We do some hiking, though it's still the height of winter at this altitude, and soak in the hot springs before Minori flies back from Kumamoto and I point the car south, back on task, heading for Satamisaki, the southernmost tip of Honshū, in Kagoshima Prefecture.

27. Satamisaki Lighthouse

Comprising the tip of Kyūshū, despite, or perhaps because of its distance from Tōkyō and Kyōto, Kagoshima has always been something of an outlier in Japan, with a fierce streak of independence running through it. Formerly called Satsuma (where oranges are the only fruit), the clan played a key role in the overthrow of the Shōgunate and the restoration of the Emperor at the head of the nation.

In more recent times, Kagoshima was the home of the Kamikaze, and today the base at Chiran acts as a museum and memorial to the men brutalised into committing suicide in the name of pride. Beliefs that these men were led by ideological fervour were dealt a blow recently when Brian Ashcraft, while researching his book on Japanese whisky, discovered a story about US troops encountering barrels marked 'whisky' that turned out to be a potent mix of alcohol, cocaine, Benzedrine and strychnine labelled with the warning 'not to be drunk until you have left Japan'. The need to prepare that level of 'Dutch courage' shows the amount of 'encouragement' the men needed to carry out their orders. Chiran is a sad place, and one that peace fans should include on their pilgrimage after Hiroshima and Nagasaki.

My first trip to Kagoshima was a joyous one. Minori and I flew to Kumamoto halfway up Kyūshū and, after a disappointing few days there, took the shinkansen to Kagoshima. I was writing my novel about Piper Alpha at the time, in which the main character is a volcanologist, and I had already half-planned for a key episode in the book to take place in Kagoshima. The city sits in the shadow of Sakurajima, a highly-active volcano that once constituted an island in the long inland sea that divides the southern tip of Kyūshū, but one particularly large eruption secured it to the mainland. It erupts an average of 800 times a year – a handful of times each day – and, like Winston Churchill at the height of the war, is permanently steaming. A layer of black ash covers everything. We rented a car and drove around the volcano, relishing the strange feeling of hopelessness that comes with the realisation of scale and importance. We stopped at a few cafés and shops and, after the coldness of Kumamoto, were delighted by the friendly welcome Kagoshimans gave us. Hearts as warm as the climate.

After Brunton's failed landing in 1868, he returned the following year on the *Sunrise*, landing on 7 July. The party, including Eliza, was hosted by the 'Prince' of the realm. Until the Meiji Restoration each domain of the Japanese state was ruled by a daimyo – a local lord – who ruled his area according to feudal traditions and strict rules imposed by the Shōgun in Edo (Tōkyō). For example, the daimyo was required to spend every second year in the capital in attendance on the Shōgun. This meant logistically that each daimyo had to maintain a residence in the city in keeping with their rank and reputation, a system designed to keep every potential challenger to the Shōgun's rule in permanent (relative) poverty. In addition, the children of the daimyo had to remain in Edo permanently, in effect hostages should the lord decide to rise up. It's a system that kept the peace for 250 years so it can be said to have been effective. In some ways the Satsuma were one of the most loyal clans. They were vehement about enforcing the ban on Christianity in Japan, for example. Yet being so far from the capital, it's easy to see in retrospect how they could come to lead a rebellion when one arose. As Britain has seen in Scotland and Japan is slowly seeing with Okinawa, distance from the centre breeds desires for independence.

The Satsuma had long been fundamentally opposed to the presence of foreigners in Japan. Their proximity to Hizen Domain may have had something to do with it: Hizen contained Nagasaki, the only port still connected to the outside world during the Edo Period, and the Hizen-Arima area was the focal point for the invasion of Christianity into Japan. As a result, the presence of foreigners had long been a local issue for the Satsuma. The Namagumi incident resulting in the death of Charles Richardson and the resulting bombardment was perhaps the nadir of relations between Satsuma and the modern world. By the time Brunton landed in Kagoshima, however, pragmatism had won out over prejudice and the party was warmly welcomed by the 'Prince'.

Their arrival was celebrated with a feast on which Brunton dwells. The food is served in the 'Western' style on Staffordshire plates and eaten with Sheffield cutlery. The editor remarks in the footnotes that this is odd since Japanese ceramics were of a very advanced and beautiful nature, but perhaps it is a sign of good hosting: if we're going to serve a 'Western' meal let's, no pun intended, go the whole hog. Besides, there's nothing people in Japan love more than buying all the equipment to complement a new hobby. You cannot take up cycling without first investing in an expensive road bike and more Lycra than should comfortably be worn by one human. Perhaps the 'Prince' of Kagoshima felt the same: If we're going to embrace 'Western' culture, we'll need all the stuff that goes with it.

Either way, it wasn't the dishes that led Brunton to bring up the feast. It was the sheer number of courses:

The striking oddity was that after every course, from soup to pastry, had been partaken of, and the meal presumably finished, a beginning was again made. Soup was once more brought on, and the other courses followed as before. Having gone through these a second time, it was evidently the host's intention to present them once more.

Brunton gets Inoue to subtly hint that no more food is required.

I too have been through this experience when I first met my in-laws. The more I ate, the more food appeared. Like a polite Sisyphus well-raised by my mother, I endeavoured to clear my plate. Like the inverse nightmare of Garfield's dream of the never-ending lasagne more food kept appearing, a culinary hydra. Eventually, embarrassed at leaving so much food, I threw in the towel before I threw up Mr Creosote style. No wafer-thin mint for me. We left an hour or so later and, in the car, loosening my belt and finally being free to belch, I asked her what the hell had just happened.

'In Japan in this kind of situation, if there is no food left at the end a meal it reflects badly on the host. It looks like they haven't bothered preparing properly for their guest.'

'So, it's not rude to stop eating?'

'No. As long as you keep eating, they'll continue serving.'

'I wish you'd told me that somewhere in the second hour of dinner.'

'I thought you were hungry.'

Like me, Brunton and his guests sat through the same dinner twice, believing in Western rules of etiquette, clearing their plate, waste-not-want-not and all that, while the Satsuma hosts were fulfilling their customary duty of serving until someone said 'when'. With no one taking control of the situation it could've gone on forever, ending in Roman-style vomiting scenes.

After all this feasting, it was time to go to work. Brunton's account of landing on the tiny island at Satamisaki is an early example of something we're more familiar with on social media – the humblebrag. Following a long paragraph describing the conditions around this rock, he casually adds that the retinue sent to accompany him 'attempt to land on the rock to join me, but failed'. He describes their boats battling the rolling waves, and the seasickness enveloping the men while, implicitly, he stands untouched by the elements. To save their blushes he returns to their ship to discuss his plans.

Work began at the turn of 1870, with a temporary light going up as early as 12 April, testament to just how much a light was needed

Satamisaki Lighthouse

there. The permanent light didn't go on until 30 November 1871.

In February 2022, after a few brief hours in a business hotel at the side of the highway, I arrive at dawn and have Satamisaki to myself. This is proper wilderness, high peaks that the road slowly winds through, hairpin after hairpin, but it's well set up. They obviously get a lot of tourists.

I walk through a long tunnel and follow the well-made path past the Misaki shrine, where I pray for the success of my venture, then climb up to the observatory. It's impossible to reach this lighthouse as it's on a little island off the coast. The tip peters out with rocks dotted like tears into the ocean and it's easy to see why they were so keen for a lighthouse here. From the observatory there's 270 degrees of view of the ocean, including the silhouette of Sakurajima in the distance. Southwards, there's nothing until Papua New Guinea.

It's like Jurassic Park, the tourist-oriented paths, signs, toilets and stairs, and the jungle-like mangrove and palm trees. I turn a corner and startle a gang of monkeys feasting on some nuts for breakfast. They look at me as if to say 'hey, we're not open to tourists yet!' and bound off into the trees. I leave them to it but keep my phone ready in case of an encounter. Although I see them many times that morning, they are always too quick and shy for a selfie.

The keeper's quarters are of the same design as the others, proving that Brunton is an 'if it ain't broke' kind of architect. While he was a stubborn bastard, he was also supremely flexible as an engineer. He had a set pattern, as the cottages show, but was able to change things as necessary for the prevailing conditions – no two of his lighthouses are the same, although patterns and styles repeat across the country.

These quarters are overrun and fallen down. The walls still stand but the roof is long gone. Weirdly the cottage is out of sight of the lighthouse and fenced off for obvious safety reasons. Considering the expense they've gone to elsewhere it's strange they haven't fixed this up. There is an information sign, however, with pictures from the early days. They built a gondola across two of the islands which must have been terrifying on calm days, and impossible in a storm. They are long gone and there doesn't seem to be a harbour, making me think it must be visited by helicopter. There's certainly no way for me to sneak out there before the information centre staff show up.

Historian James Holland talks about walking the ground, how visiting battlefields gives you a good sense of things and can help answer questions about why things were done a certain way. Being able to immerse yourself in the atmosphere of the place as well as the project is important. Snatched moments and day trip visits are great when that's all there is but being able to spend weeks thinking about nothing else is good. I'm glad I took this trip, despite my fears.

The waves are picking up, whiter and whiter. There's a tear across the sky like the nexus in *Generations*, and the weather is going to turn at some point. I don't want to leave yet, having all this to myself. However, I'm growing tired after ten days on the road, and this translates into a restlessness, a need to keep moving homewards. A sign confirms this as the most southerly point of Japan's 'home islands' (Honshū, Kyūshū, Shikoku and Hokkaidō). Wakkanai is the northernmost, Nemuro is the most easterly, Sasebo is in the west. I've been to all but Wakkanai, so there's another name for the travel bucket list. I'm at the turning point, heading north, Gifu the target. I've got one lighthouse left on this trip: Tsurushima. The end is in sight.

28. *Tsurushima Lighthouse*

The next lighthouse is in Shikoku and the easiest way there is by ferry. My plan was to catch the ferry from Beppu, one of Japan's most famous hot spring spots. I went there about ten years ago with Dan and Robert, and Mike who lived in Matsuyama. We had a few baths and drank a lot of beer, so much so that we had a panicked scramble for the ferry the next day that ended with four large foreigners, each with backpacks, squishing into the back of a single taxi, pissing themselves laughing. There's also a ferry from Usuki, which is further south and a new place for me, so I alter plans and drive there. This turns out to have been the best decision of the trip.

Usuki is a small castle town, so small I'd never heard of it before but what a secret to keep! A preserved old town open to tourists but not ruined in the name of capitalism. Beautiful winding streets, friendly people, and a relaxed, unpretentious vibe. Cool little coffee shops, a wide selection of eateries, locals arts and crafts. I'm beginning to see this a lot in small towns across Japan. At first glance it looks like gentrification and it is in a way, but not a class thing, a generational thing. The twenty- and thirty-year-olds are flexing their entrepreneurial muscles and opening the kinds of businesses they wish they could frequent. The old person's coffee shop selling 'mornings' and stinking of smoke are giving way to clean, airy cafés with sustainably-sourced coffee, craft beer and craft burgers. For Europeans and Americans this may not sound that impressive or that welcome but in Japan, where the elderly, by dint of superior numbers, are king, everything has been catered towards them. Now fresh life is being breathed into dying towns – not replacing, but coexisting – and it's the change itself that's refreshing, a new lick of paint. Optimism.

I ride the ferry, drive into Matsuyama where apparently no one has ever heard of the state of emergency. It's jumping, buzzing, lights and music and people. I don't have the energy. Instead, I have an early night, not looking forward to the next day. Tsurushima will be an ordeal. It's the last lighthouse of the trip, the last one west of Gifu, and the most infuriating: The only ferry out is at 9.10 am and there isn't one back until 4.02 pm. I'm on the island for the day. Like Mutsurejima, but worse. There's nothing on the island beyond a few houses and a lot of orange trees.

Tsurushima Lighthouse is on the northern end of the island, about halfway up looking out over a busy shipping lane feeding Matsuyama and funnelling through the inland sea connecting the Pacific coast of Japan. A map shows the area that the light covers, a roughly 100-degree arc stretching from Yashiro island in the east to Nobutsuna in the west. There's a certain efficiency in this since the light not only warns about the location of Tsurushima – at that time uninhabited – but it would show enough of the other islands to invalidate the need for more than one lighthouse. Engineering genius.

Construction began in September 1871, and the light was illuminated on 15 June 1873. The keeper's cottages and storehouses were done by July. A plaque nearby erected by Matsuyama City goes into great detail about the cottage. Between 1995 and 1997 the buildings were restored to their original appearance using all original materials, including imported glass on the windows (which are sadly covered by storm shutters, though I'm not sure I could tell the difference between domestic and imported glass). The floorboards are of Japanese cypress, and there are four fireplaces, roughly in each corner, feeding into a chimney at either end. Flanked on two sides by orange groves ('tis the season) and built into the mountain to protect it from the wind. Even the outside toilets have been preserved.

The plaque claims, and who am I to argue, that this is the only one hundred per cent original lighthouse complex in Japan, without any remodelling or what it snarkily refers to as 'mock-Western' style popular in the Meiji era. It does admit that the roof was quickly remodelled after building – the initial roof would have been sloped in one direction, rather than the current 'hipped' design. The roof is, in fact, reminiscent of a Japanese temple roof, and with tiles rather than the slate an Aberdonian would expect on granite buildings such as these. It's an interesting blend of Scottish and Japanese design.

Foreign lighthouse keepers lived here until January 1876, after which local keepers took over. It became unmanned in April 1963. It's perfectly peaceful, nothing but birdsong and the thrum of ferries going to and from all the other islands, never here. It's a clear, crisp day, about four degrees but there's no wind so it's not too cold. It's a little after 10 am and I'm done. The ferry is not for another six hours.

I circumnavigate the island twice. I sit and watch the sea from all four compass points. I transcribe an interview I conducted a few weeks previously. I chat with anyone who'll talk to me but the local dialect is so thick and fast I am quickly lost. Everyone else is there to work on the oranges, so beyond simple curiosity, they have little interest in entertaining me. I vaguely hope someone will say, 'I'm just hopping over to the mainland, fancy a lift?' but nothing comes. I'm stuck here and my phone battery is about to die.

Hours later, back on Shikoku, I drive to Marugame and check into a cheap business hotel. Before dawn I'll take a local ferry to Hiroshima Island where Frank Toovey Lake is buried. Before heading to Hiroshima, I have a Zoom chat with Graham Thomas, the man who wrote the book on Lake's grave.

'I met my wife, Satoko, in Tōkyō but she is from Kagawa and her mother's family are from Hiroshima,' he tells me. 'They still keep a holiday home there. There's a monk living in it at the moment.

'The second or third time we went to visit her family, we went over to the island with Satoko's father. We were driving back to pick up the ferry and he suddenly said, 'I want to show you something'. I couldn't quite understand what it was, just that it was some sort of grave. However, he couldn't find it and had to ask for directions.

'You'll have seen in the book I wrote that there are pictures from the first time I saw it. The fundamental thing about it then is that all the information on the sign was completely wrong. I was fascinated by the mystery and surprised by the existence of the grave. How on Earth did he end up here? Why wasn't he buried at sea or taken elsewhere?

'When I returned to the UK in 2003 I then had easy access to the National Archives so I did the research. But because of the misinformation the first time, I went and got the logbook – the

National Archives have a huge collection of logbooks going right back – on the sign at the grave it said HMS *Sylvia*, so I went to the archives, got out the logbook and found absolutely nothing. No Lake. No record of death. No burial at all. And deaths are always recorded. So, I went to the list of vessels in the China squadron, which was the name of RN squadron in that part of the world at that time, and I literally went through all the vessels. Some I could discount quickly because it was clear they had nothing to do with Japan, but the rest I just had to get the bloody logbooks out. But doing that I found so much amazing material – hand drawn maps – so many of the ships stopped at Hiroshima, and you have every part of the route in huge detail... so I just kept doing this. It took me years to try and unravel the story and it was only through luck, actually, through reading Brunton's autobiography, that the whole mystery unravelled. I hadn't really thought about Brunton before. In the National Archive there was a small section of books about him, and I was just bored of looking at lists of bloody sailors so I went through some of the books and there was this paragraph of him talking about going to the island. Although he doesn't name Lake, he says he was there and that a seaman died and described the funeral. It all fell into place. Having found it I had to completely reconstruct everything because HMS *Manilla* does have a logbook and it was all in there.'

'And we know the logbook is reliable,' I say, 'because Brunton didn't get anywhere near it!'

'I've never been able to find definitive evidence about how he died but I think it most likely is that he got cholera when they were in the Kobe area. And if it was cholera, they wouldn't want to keep the body. And I've certainly seen in other ships' logs there were burials at sea, so for him to have been buried on land is unusual. But having said that, why on Earth did the islanders seem reasonably happy at having these foreigners turn up and bury somebody. Hiroshima then was a stopover point in the Inland Sea where water could be taken on, so foreign ships would stop in the bay regularly, so there was this constant connection, they were of benefit to the local economy.

'In Enoura, close to the grave there's a junior high school which closed a while ago. Three years ago, it became a municipal office and there is a little exhibition about the grave and the history of the island. We put up a new plaque at the grave and added the Brunton connection, and about a year after that was unveiled, the Coastguard did their own ceremony at the graveside to celebrate Brunton because they have a fundamental appreciation of what Brunton did. They were quite interested, appreciative that somebody had made a reference to Brunton and something celebrating him and his life.

'The grave has been looked after, which is one of the fascinating things, that people have been looking after it since 1868.'

I'm out and back just as the sun is coming out. The way the ferries work I can either spend twenty minutes on the island or most of the day. After Tsurushima, I'm not up to it. I leg it from the terminal to the grave which, thanks to Graham, I find without any problem, and leg it back, just in time. I get odd looks, this foreigner taking the first ferry of the day to the mainland – has he been here all night? How did no one know? – but this is a commuter ferry and no one is in a chatty mood this early on a work day.

Back on the road I make a quick detour to Shikoku Mura, an open-air museum like Meiji Mura, where they have the transferred and rebuilt keepers' quarters from Esaki and Nabeshima. I wander around taking photos but this is it, the last day. I can be home before dinner if I step on it. So I do.

29. *Tsurugisaki Lighthouse*

Tsurugisaki keeps slipping my mind. In all my calculations I only have two more lighthouses to visit: Mikomotoshima and Kinkasan. Thankfully, I marked each one on Google Maps when I began this project, and one little heart south of Yokohama catches my eye.

It's been a year since Jason and I went to Izu. In that time he's had a son. Another year of Covid, but things are starting to loosen up and my Kyūshū trip went without a hitch, so we decide to go back, this time as families. We arrange to meet at the villas, and as I'm on holiday and Minori isn't yet, I head off a day early, that heart in Kanagawa taunting me.

I leave around 3 am, fire down the highway and reach Yokosuka around breakfast time. Yokosuka is the home of the US forces on Honshū, about 25,000 troops are stationed there, another remnant of the occupation that no one wants and no one wants to pay to replace with domestic troops. Everything filtered through an increasingly aggressive China.

Miura, the tip of the peninsula, seems to be where Yokohamans come to play. A mile-long stretch of gorgeous beach, the water at this time already packed with windsurfers and jet skis. I crawl along, seemingly the only one not searching for a parking space, and eventually break on through to the other side. As always, the roads narrow, disappear. I wind between fields, the teasing peak of the lighthouse briefly visible then gone. A handwritten sign points to a car park though it looks much more like a junkyard. Old bicycles, piles of rusting metal, boxes of plastic bottles and a platoon of mangy cats. Two old men lounge in amongst it all, and the smell of drink on the one who comes to the car for his fee is overpowering at this time. This is decidedly not a tourist attraction.

The sea smell again, salt and ions, seaweed and rot. This is a fishing point, paths down to the rocks, rods pointed out to sea, a sunny spring Sunday morning perfect for it. I stay on the paved road, follow it to the lighthouse.

Tsurugisaki has seen better days. The sign above the door decaying and almost unreadable, the foundations of the quarters filled in and broken again. The lighthouse has a strange lintel I don't remember seeing on any of the others, and the tower is octagonal rather than round, with the buildings on the back rather than either side. A circle of daffodils seems to be the only sign of care. The radar station overwhelms everything. The sign doesn't mention Brunton, just the basic facts: 17 m tall, 41 m above sea level. 1 March 1871.

Tsurugisaki Lighthouse

After all that driving, nearly six hours on the road, I kind of expect more, though I shouldn't now. There's a feeling of anticlimax, a box ticked. I wander around for five or ten minutes thinking of something to say. My hay fever is bad, that's about it.

I follow a path down to the rocks where the fishermen sit. They eye me, but I don't have any gear so I'm not going to muscle in on their favourite spots. The path is non-existent and I get mud all up my leg. The rocks are fascinating, canyons carved by the sea, towers, caves, pools. A couple of families with small kids lift rocks and splash. The lighthouse is at the highest point but the rocks jut out much further. I follow the valleys and soon I'm standing between the lighthouse and the sea, a strange place to be, the first time I've seen a lighthouse from this angle without being on an opposing shore. Of course, this is the face of the lighthouse, the way it looks at the world. I'm used to seeing them from the back, looking over their shoulder, the view from their perspective. One thing I'd like to experience is seeing one of them, lit at night, from the deck of a ship that's crossed the ocean. The land ho! experience, the welcoming side of a lighthouse.

I leave, the two old men ignoring me now I'm not their concern. I follow the coast round, think about stopping at Enoshima for lunch but the crowds are unbelievable. It's the first warm weekend of the year and every available space is filled with cars from Yokohama, Kawasaki, Tōkyō. I keep going, and keep going, arriving in Mishima mid-afternoon. Tomorrow morning Minori will take the shinkansen, I'll pick her up and we'll drive to Hakone for an onsen over-looking Fuji; visiting hot spring resorts is one of the most quintessential Japanese experiences that I, unaccountably, haven't done.

Now, if my calculations are correct: two to go, the big ones, the hardest, the adventures. I'm nearing the end and wondering if it's all been worth it.

A few months later, my mother-in-law, Miyoko, asks about these trips and I mention going to Miura.

'My family originally came from there,' she says, jumping up and rifling through some papers on the sideboard.

'I thought they were from Gujō?'

'Yes, but originally...where is it?'

I look at Minori who shrugs. 'Her family are descended from a famous samurai family.'

'Really?' I perk up but Minori doesn't seem that excited. One of those things she's heard since she was a kid.

'Here it is.' Miyoko pulls out a clipping from the local newspaper, the *Chunichi Shimbun* from 2005. The page has seen better days, is yellowing and frayed around the edges. I handle it carefully, squinting at the kanji trying to make it out. Miyoko explains.

'Miura is where the Miura clan are from. They are an old samurai family connected to the Taira clan.'

Them, I've heard of. The Taira were one of the families that ruled Japan from the Heian period (8th century). Their great rivals were the Minamoto who eventually destroyed the clan in 1180. The Minamoto were known by another name: Genji, as in *The Tale of*. The story is the subject of the *Heike Monogatari*, one of the classics of Japanese literature (Heike is another name for the Taira). The Miura, it seems, are a branch of the Taira who supported Minamoto no Yoritomo, the great Minamoto leader, in 1180 and ruled the Miura Peninsula until 1247 when they were destroyed by the Hōjō.

'Those who survived fled, led by the only surviving brother, Iemura, chased by the Hōjō. They had roots in this area so they came here.'

The article shows how they followed the Kiso River to Yaotsu and turned north. Miyoko herself is from Yaotsu, the wider family spread out between there and Gujō.

I'm fascinated, these little connections, coincidences throwing up stories. Minori looks bored. 'It doesn't mean anything. It's not like we're actually part of this great family.' Go back far enough and everyone's related to everyone else.

Miyoko ignores her. It's something interesting, something unique. A trail through history, footsteps on a map. Some small piece of DNA, some drop of blood that connects back to people in *The Tale of Heike* and *The Tale of Genji*.

30. *Mikomotoshima Lighthouse*

After Hakone, Minori and I drive down to Shimoda and meet up with Jason, Haruna and Hikaru, their new son. On the first night we have a barbecue, the two families in neighbouring villas. At 3 am, Jason and I set off to meet the fishing charter that would drop us off at Mikomotoshima, a sleepy drive to Shimoda Harbour while the wives sleep on. A brusque but kindly old sea dog gives us the absolute minimal amount of information and leaves us slightly confused standing before his boat. When the other fishermen - baffled by the two foreigners, only one of which has fishing tackle - get on board, we follow. The gangplank is literally a piece of wood at a 65-degree angle. Jason clambers up using all four limbs and I pass the gear to him, then follow with even less grace. We take our places with seven bemused fishermen, three younger than us, the rest around retirement age, and head out to sea, a straight line the 11 km to Mikomotoshima, hanging onto our hats the whole way. It takes about half an hour. As we approach, the captain calls to us to prepare to land. Only us. The other seven passively watch. He gets us to stand on the open prow and, as it touches the top of a cliff, bouncing up and down with the waves, tells us to jump.

'I'll be back at two.' He sails off with the other seven fishermen.

'You think he'll be back?'

'We'll find out one way or the other.'

'Oh well.'

We clamber up the rocks towards the lighthouse and I feel a bit like Jim Hawkins as we crest the ridge and see the island curve in a crescent away from us. There are three peaks to Mikomotoshima, roughly in a line along the crescent ridge. The lighthouse stands to our right, the central peak to our immediate left, and a final peak beyond that with some sort of monument at the top. Below us is a natural inlet that's been turned at some point into a small harbour, presumably for the lighthouse. That would be where Brunton had come ashore. We carry our gear up to the lighthouse and are relieved to see the boat circling the island and dropping the others off at different points, presumably depending on their preferences for fishing spots.

This lighthouse was the first to go up, with ground broken in April 1869 with a temporary light on 10 November 1869. It was permanently illuminated on 1 January 1871, a fact commemorated by the rusting sign above the door. It's 23.3 m tall, standing 39 m above sea level.

More than any other I've been to so far, this is not a tourist destination. There are no signs, no QR codes, no explanations. Just the lighthouse tall and sturdy, thick black bands around its white body. There's no doubt this was built to last, built to withstand the worst the Pacific Ocean could throw at it, and it has. Below, in the lee of the hill, are the cottages and storehouses. The cottages are locked up, storerooms these days, with a helipad to one side. The old storerooms and toilets are falling down, rubble everywhere. If you don't look after things out here, they'll very quickly be destroyed.

It's windy but warm. I circle, taking photos, collecting rocks. We're here for nine hours with no toilet and so the harbour coffee was a bad idea. Jason goes hunting for a good fishing spot but we realise quickly why no one came to fish on this side of the island – it's surrounded by seaweed which catch his lures and won't give them back.

Exhausted but happy, we settle into the lee of a dry-stone wall and a rock formation and doze off.

The day passes like this. One of us napping, the other off exploring. One of us reading, the other sleeping. One of us taking photos while the other tries to find somewhere secluded-but-safe to answer the calls of nature. I climb all the peaks, and discover the monument is a stone to all the unknown sailors lost at sea, a sobering reminder of what all of this means, why all of this matters.

This is the longest I've spent on one of these islands, the longest and the most remote, but the time passes. Having a friend here changes everything. On Tsurushima I was alone with my thoughts. Here, even napping, Jason is a companion, the kind of friend who you don't need to fill silence with, that you can just be yourself with. Is this what I left Scotland in search of because I never truly found it there? Perhaps that's where the alienation came from, from never finding friends I could totally relax with? Not because they didn't exist, because I have close friends from Scotland, but because of who I was when I met them. They got to know me when I was at my most broken and they remember me that way. I love them for that but the person they think I am has long gone. When I see them now, they aren't seeing me, they are seeing the old me. Jason didn't know that Iain, but we recognise it in each other.

The hours pass idle, idyllic. The boat comes back, and we greet him like an old friend. On the dock Minori, Haruna and Hikaru wait, waving, welcoming us home.

31. *Back in Britain*

Brunton was given a final audience with the Emperor, a farewell dinner and a parting bonus of 2,000 yen (about £500 at the time). Pedlar notes that regarding Brunton's termination, 'It is still not clear why this was done and many people criticised the way his contract was so suddenly terminated'. At the time, maybe those, particularly Parkes, who shared Brunton's view of the bureaucracy and the reliability of Japanese workers were unhappy but looking both at the historical trends of the time, the original intentions of the yatoi scheme, and the fact that Brunton had burned a lot of bridges along the way, it doesn't seem quite so surprising. Brunton's disdain aside, he had trained his immediate replacement impeccably. Fujikura Kentatsu took over upon Brunton's departure and did an excellent job. While Brunton's lighthouses were the first, work didn't stop when he left. The graveyards, as they say, are full of people who thought they were irreplaceable. Unlike Dyer, Brunton received no honours. Griffis, in his introduction, points out that the Bureau of Decorations hadn't then been formed (although decorations and honours existed before the Bureau was formalised, so they could have given him something if they had felt so inclined) but he also notes that Brunton was unlikely to receive much in the way of honour from those he had so strongly and regularly criticised. Politics is politics the world over.

According to Brunton his final tally was 'thirty-seven oceans lights, nine harbour lights, three light vessels, fifteen buoys, and eight beacons'. He set sail on 10 March 1876 on board the *Oceanic* bound for San Francisco. After one last salvo against the iniquities of the Japanese, signing off with a note of bitterness and the unmistakable scent of racism, Brunton's memoir is done. Presumably, he crossed the continental US. McVean and Blundell left Japan exactly a month later, on the *Belgie*, heading in the same direction. While searching for passenger records I toyed with the tantalising possibility that the three men who left Britain together returned in each other's company. I fervently hoped it was true, my imagination running away with itself. I even began sketching out an idea for a play, the three engineers cooped up in a steamer on the Pacific with nothing to do but go over eight years of ill-feeling and recriminations. It wasn't to be, but I couldn't help wondering whether McVean and Blundell delayed their departure by a month precisely to avoid this situation.

On his return to Britain he presented his paper 'The Japan Lights' to the Institute of Civil Engineers and began job hunting. In some ways, however, Brunton's life was over. He'd lived the highlight of his obituary and from here slipped back into obscurity. In 1878 he took on the position of manager at Young's Paraffin Oil Company in Glasgow, and the 1881 census has the Bruntons living in Bathgate. The daughters, Mary and Harriet are fourteen and eleven, and listed as scholars. Also included in the household are two servants. That year he presented a paper on 'The Production of Paraffin and Paraffin Oils' to the Institute of Civil Engineers. All of his papers are reproduced in the Cortazzi edition of this memoirs.

He went into business for himself producing 'architectural ornamentation' and solved 'some of the difficult problems of acoustics in theatres and public halls' marking a reconnection with his family's theatrical roots. The family moved to London where he continued to work on various projects as an architect and engineer.

In his final years he completed the manuscript of his memoirs, which he snappily titled *The Awakening of a Nation: being a description of the entry of Japan into the Sisterhood of Nations, with an Elucidation of the Character of the People from personal experience.* It was in two parts, forming a history of the country followed by his own story. The first part was never published.

After his death the manuscript ended up with Charlotte C Stoper, a writer and Shakespeare scholar who was a friend of the family. In Weldon's 1938 introduction, he describes how Stoper could do nothing with the manuscript to make it publishable. At the turn of the year from 1905 to 1906 Dr William Elliot Griffis, an American scholar and Japanophile, met Eliza Brunton and Charlotte

Stoper in England. He bought the manuscript and the rights from 'the hard-pressed widow'. When Griffis died in 1928 the book which he had by now heavily edited was no closer to publication and passed into Rutgers University Library. In 1938, re-edited by Fredrick Weldon, the book was finally published as *Schoolmaster to an Empire*.

In 1991, on the 150th anniversary of Brunton's birth, two editions were published, *Schoolmaster to an Empire*, re-re-edited by Edward R Beauchamp, and *Building Japan 1868-1876* based on Griffis's edits. Beauchamp's is a more complete version of the memoir while the Griffis edition contains a detailed appendix complete with papers, letters and other useful documents.

Brunton died of a brain haemorrhage on 24 April 1901 aged fifty-nine. He was living in South Kensington at the time and is buried at West Norwood Cemetery.

32. *Kinkasan Lighthouse*

Five years after this whole thing started, Minori and I pick up the rental car from Hanamaki Airport in Iwate and head south-east for Miyagi. At this stage it's still unclear exactly how I can get to Kinkasan Lighthouse, or whether I even can. We are travelling on a prayer.

Kinkasan, as I said at the beginning, was once a popular destination, an inhabited island with enough tourism to keep it ticking over. In 2011 the tsunami ended all of that. Today, most of the island is wild, uninhabitable. A skeleton staff stay on at Kinkasan Temple but no one else lives there now. As a result, it's not geared up for visitors. There's a regular ferry, if once a week can be described as regular. It's possible to stay at the temple. It's tantalisingly possible.

Kinkasan Lighthouse

The shrine and port are on the north-western side of the island. The lighthouse is on the south-east point. There used to be a road around the island linking them but the tsunami washed that away and it hasn't been rebuilt. There is a hiking trail over the mountain and on the shrine side it's well tended. Over the hill, however, it's fallen into disrepair. There is a lot of information online, all of it out of date. A month before we caught our flight, I emailed the shrine staff. They were non-committal in that bureaucratic Japanese way where they try to put you off without actually saying no. It's technically possible to hike to the lighthouse, they told me. Technically. But it can't be done in a day.

It can be done in a day. The distances are not nothing: 10 to 15 km depending on how you go. I've hiked longer, further, harder. Perhaps what they mean is that it can't be done in a day with the current ferry schedule. They must be angling for me to book a night. I email back to make a reservation. They never reply.

The next option is just to chance it: I have a tiny ridge tent. I can take the ferry, load myself up for the night and wild camp beside the lighthouse. Google Maps shows the area around the lighthouse to be a flat meadow-like spit of land. At the height of summer it'll be warm enough, dry enough, and won't be dark for all that long at night. Again, I've camped in worse places, at worse times of the year. This to me is the most appealing, the most romantic, and what a final chapter, lying beneath the stars as the light sweeps over the ocean.

The final option is the easiest and the most expensive – there are whale watching and fishing charters from nearby Ayukawa Port. For a fee, one of them will take me wherever I want to go. Biggest drawback: there is nowhere to land on the lighthouse side – access by helicopter only and I don't have that kind of money.

Minori decides she's coming with me so wild camping is out. Part of me is disappointed but it simplifies things. We book into a ryokan in Matsushima, an hour or so from Ayukawa, for three nights and wait to see what the weather will do. The rainy season has gone on almost an extra month, and we're close to typhoon season. I need to be flexible. Once we're checked in I call the fishing charter

Sea Dream Kinkasan. He's a nice guy, very helpful, gives a bit of advice, the next day's forecast is good, so we're booked. We spend the evening in Matsushima eating beef tongue sausages and rewriting the famous Matsushima haiku, often attributed to Bashō, to our own taste:

松島やああ牛タンや瓶ビールや
Matsushima ya
Aa gyu-tan ya
Bin biru ya

There's something mildly decadent about chartering your own ship. It's not crazy expensive – I'm not chartering a yacht in the Caribbean – but we're both from families of modest means so just the idea seems outlandish. The cost of visiting this lighthouse alone is likely to outweigh any advance I get for this book, but this project has long since outstripped any kind of sense. A staff of three accompanies us out into the Pacific dawn, gulls circling, the water flat, deep, dark. One man, gold chain, open shirt, takes the wheel. The guy I spoke to on the phone joins us in the back. The woman tosses scraps at the gulls. I explain to them what we're doing and why.

'We take people round here quite regularly,' he says. 'With a dinghy you can land. It's dangerous and we don't recommend it, but it's possible.'

I'm about to demand to be provided with a dinghy when Minori asks something much more sensible: why?

'People love bouldering here. Bouldering and rope climbing. The cliffs are covered with routes. Did you know they name the route after the first person who climbed it?'

'Yes,' says Minori. 'I do bouldering.' Now she's gearing up to demand a dinghy.

'Oh really? Have you ever heard of Treasure Island as a bouldering site?'

'Yeah, the name rings a bell.'

'That's what they call this place. The first kanji, *kin*, means gold, so they call it Treasure Island.'

My Robert Louis Stevenson radar goes into hyperdrive. The final lighthouse in my Brunton project is on Treasure Island. Give me a dinghy, a tent, and supplies right now! I explain my original idea to him, of hiking, of maybe camping.

'You shouldn't,' he says. 'We took a guy over yesterday who hiked to the lighthouse.'

I feel like crying.

'He was stung by a suzumebachi [murder hornet], half-a-dozen leeches attached themselves to him, he fell twice and only narrowly avoided going over the cliffs, he cut his leg pretty badly. Look.'

He shows me some photos on his phone. The guy is retired, but clearly fit. His face is marked with red welts, as are his arms, from the leeches. His forearm has a nasty red mark, all swollen and raw, the bee sting. He looks a wreck, lucky to be alive.

'See,' Minori says. 'That could have been you.'

'See,' I say. 'That could have been me. He made it!'

We take photos and videos from all the angles possible. I'm seeing this land as Brunton would have, from the sea, bobbing in the swell. He never saw this lighthouse finished, was long gone by the time it was lit.

Work began in early 1874, so it would have been underway during his final tour, and it was finished and illuminated on 1 November 1876, the last one to go up. In fact, Brunton's last lighthouse was lit just as he was making his final presentation to the Institute of Civil Engineers. Made of granite, it stands 56.4 m above sea level, where we bob around, snapping away. Apparently, the US Navy destroyed it during World War Two, and it was rebuilt to the original design afterwards, becoming fully automated in 2005. So it didn't survive the war, but it survived the tsunami, despite being right in harm's way.

The coastline, the rest of the island weren't so lucky. Huge bites have been taken out of the cliffs. The sections that somehow escaped ravaging only serve to throw the rest into sharp relief. It's like when the tide collapses a sandcastle, except these walls tower above us, gone in an instant. From this angle it strangely reminds me of the island in *Battle Royale* and I idly wonder where that was filmed.

It's been eleven years since the tsunami but vegetation is only now beginning to return. This coastline is famous for its pine trees. Matsushima, one of Japan's three most beautiful views, is literally named after them – Matsushima translating as 'pine tree islands' – but today Kinkasan is covered in saplings encased in protective blue plastic to keep them safe from the deer that roam the island. While we're taking photos of the lighthouse, the woman is taking photos of the coastline, writing down numbers and notes. I want to ask about the tsunami, to hear their stories, but I don't. If they offer information, great, but you don't quiz people about their trauma without permission. It isn't that kind of relationship, that kind of mood. This is business.

'Do you want to visit the shrine?'

'Can we?'

'Sure, it's your ship.'

'They say if you visit three times within the same year, you'll never have money problems again,' says the woman.

'I don't think we can manage three times in one year.'

'No,' she laughs. 'I think that's the point.'

They leave us for half an hour and we stroll around. I buy all kinds of souvenirs and charms from the shrine, contributing to what I hope will one day be a new road. Nearby are the ruins of a hotel, once thriving they say, a big European-looking building high above the sea with beautiful views of the mainland, now a gutted shell, its insides ripped out by the waves. I've seen some islands decimated by economics, by the march of progress, by demographics, but never one that was destroyed in an instant. The horror of it is too vivid, too clear, the scars naked.

We sail back melancholy. The project is done, all twenty-two lighthouses bagged, give or take a kilometre or two. I expected elation. I nearly packed something fizzy with a cork. Instead the tsunami haunts me.

Driving back we pass concrete walls, plains denuded of all but rock, salt-sown land now useless. Warning signs, sirens, evacuation towers that look too flimsy, too low, too hopeful. I follow the roads without any real sense of destination. It's late morning still, and I need to let my mind wander.

The road winds north up the coast. On that first trip five years earlier I camped somewhere around here. I stopped at Matsushima tourist information who pointed me to a campsite that turned out to be ninety minutes away. I was exhausted, in the grip of a fever I later realised was due to thirty-six bee stings from a campground in Fukushima. I drove these roads then but remember nothing. Somewhere up ahead, much further north, is the lone pine tree, Ipponmatsu, a symbol to the dead, the sole survivor of tens of thousands of pines washed away. Beside it the shell of an elementary school. It's so easy to forget when it's out of sight at the other end of the country.

We are silent in the car. No music. No chat. Both with our thoughts. We are lucky, both of us, our families healthy, alive, flourishing. Neither of us has experienced trauma on this scale, anything the press would call a tragedy. I've spent a large part of my life trying to understand trauma, writing first about the Piper Alpha disaster, later doing a PhD on the representation of trauma and treatment, immersing myself in the theory, but it's all theory. Understanding the 'Why', not the 'What'. Here, laid out before us, all around us, is the 'What'.

We crest a hill and below is the town of Onagawa. I recognise this. Remember this view. I pull in beside a sign that says something like, 'Historical Tsunami Inundation Point: End'. This is where the waters reached. Below us, the entire town of Onagawa, the port, a funnel of mountains pointing out to sea. We get out, sit on the bonnet and look down at a town not one building of which is more than eleven years old, and cry.

33. *Onagawa*

We drive into Onagawa for lunch. From the shoreline they've built a new shopping complex, a long street, wooden decking, wooden buildings each housing a local business: a diving shop, pizza restaurant, coffee shop, a guitar shop, seafood, seafood, seafood. We spend liberally, eat too much, trying to pump some money into the economy here. I take my coffee and sit on the steps people-watching. I don't know if it's me but there seems to be a sombreness to the town. Children are playing but they aren't the riot of noise and energy kids usually are. Couples hold hands, something you rarely see in Japan. The restaurants are peopled by generations, wheelchair-bound grandmothers to pushchair-bound babies. I see the quiet strength in the faces of growing families, the old people eating sashimi, the new businesses thriving. The reminders are everywhere, a polished propellor, a hefty anchor turned into public art, the past incorporated into the present, but people are getting on with the business of existence. Maybe it's me, maybe it's my mood. Projecting it onto this place. What else would I expect on a Monday at lunchtime? A festival? An Austin Powers opening sequence?

At the waterfront, the destroyed remains of the police station turned into a memorial. A piece of art, a flag pole, curved at the top like a street light, but with two bronze children perched on top pointing out to sea. A bell, rope hanging, ready to be rung. Always ready. Photos of before and after. And the stats, the bare facts of it: The tsunami struck at 2.46 pm precisely on 11 March 2011, the 23rd year of the Heisei era. 827 dead. A further twenty-two died later from complications and injuries. 3,934 houses destroyed. 1,631 other buildings. And the trauma. How do you calculate the trauma?

It was never my intention to end the journey on the Sanriku Coast. Logistically, this was a mistake. Kinkasan should have been the first or second lighthouse. I had the idea on my trip to Tōhoku five years ago. I visited Shiriyazaki in Aomori, a few hours north of here, saw that the idea had legs and ran with it. Looking at the map, I'd thought Kyūshū would be the end. North to south. Logical, right? Or maybe Mikomotoshima, the one I'd been told would be the hardest. Sitting on the dock of the bay in Onagawa, ropes ringing against masts, the clatter of a fishing industry, the buzz of Harleys pulling in to the roadside station, I can't imagine having finished anywhere else.

For all the images I had of lighthouses – romantic, thrilling, dangerous, challenging – it's taken the reality of the tsunami to make me understand what they really are: symbols to our frailty. Our fragility. Humans may be the dominant species but this planet can humble us in seconds. The lighthouse is an acknowledgement of that, an attempt to use our intellect in service to our survival. By putting the lights here we can save lives. Without them, a ship hits a submerged rock and all hands are lost. These lights have saved countless thousands, tens, hundreds of thousands of lives but they are useless when the planet steps things up. A tsunami cannot be stopped. The memorial museum in Ishinomaki is stark: this will happen again.

34. *Epilogue*

What does it matter what kind of man Richard Henry Brunton was? It matters, but it isn't everything. He was a hard man to like; a man who saved thousands of lives. He is a hero and someone who should not be raised onto a pedestal. What have I learned about Henry Brunton over these five years of trailing him around the coast of Japan?

That life is fragile. Humans are frail. Over these five years we've had Covid. I've moved firmly into what I hope will be middle age. I've began to take notice of mortality. Henry Brunton thought Japan was his first step towards greatness, but in his late twenties, his early thirties, he'd already peaked. We look to the future while ignoring the present and only notice when we see the shape of the past. Henry Brunton slipped into obscurity soon after leaving Yokohama. He kept working. His family prospered. But he wasn't to be a great man, an eminent man. His memoirs were never published because he had little new to say about Japan, and what he did say was often objectionable. In his homeland, few have ever heard of him.

He died young by our standards, a little shy of his 60th birthday. How did he feel? Was he bitter? I can certainly imagine so. He was a man given to bitterness, to grudges and resentments. He was explicit in wanting his name linked to the lighthouses, added to the announcements to shipping, to the plaques. He wanted immortality. He never achieved the fame of the Stevensons, or the infamy of Glover. He did his job, went home, and that was that. Not a great life. Not an eminent life. But an important life. An important legacy. Kinkasan Lighthouse is still standing after a tsunami. It took an atomic bomb to knock down Iojima Lighthouse. Technology will eventually replace them all but Henry Brunton did his bit for the cause of human frailty and that's pretty great in my book.

Bibliography and Sources

BOOKS

W G Beasley, *The Meiji Restoration* (1972)

Isabella Bird, *Unbeaten Tracks in Japan* (2010)

Ardath W Burks, *The Modernizers: Overseas Students, Foreign Employees, and Meiji Japan* (2021)

Richard Henry Brunton, *Building Japan 1868-1876* (1991)

Richard Henry Brunton, *Schoolmaster to an Empire: Richard Henry Brunton in Meiji Japan, 1868-1876* (1991)

Kunitake Kume (*et al*), *Japan Rising: The Iwakura Embassy to the USA and Europe 1871-1873* (2009)

Janice P Nimura, *Daughters of the Samurai: A Journey from East to West and Back* (2015)

Neil Pedlar, *The Imported Pioneers: Westerners Who Helped Build Modern Japan* (1990)

Burritt Sabin, *A Historical Guide to Yokohama: Sketches of the Twice-risen Phoenix* (2002)

Sir Ernest Satow, *A Diplomat in Japan: The Inner History of the Critical Years in the Evolution of Japan When the Ports Were Opened and the Monarchy Restored* (2015)

Yokohama Kaikō Shiryōkan, *Richard H Brunton: Father of Japan Lights and Yokohama Urban Planning* (1991)

Graham Thomas, *A Hiroshima Grave: A 150-Year Long Story* (2013)

WEBSITES

Berkshire History - https://www.berkshirehistory.com

Graces Guide - https://www.gracesguide.co.uk/Main_Page

History Hub - https://historyhub.history.gov/welcome

Norfolk Tales Myths - https://norfolktalesmyths.com

Oxford Dictionary of National Biography - https://www.oxforddnb.com

Regency Redingote - https://regencyredingote.wordpress.com

RootsWeb - https://home.rootsweb.com

The Scots Magazine - https://www.scotsmagazine.com

Yokohama Archives of History - http://www.kaikou.city.yokohama.jp/en/index.html

FURTHER READING

Ian Buruma, *Wages of Guilt: Memories of War in Germany & Japan* (2015)

Amy Chavez, *The Widow, The Priest, and the Octopus Hunter* (2022)

John Dougill, *In Search of Japan's Hidden Christians* (2012)

Chris Glenn, *The Battle of Sekigahara: The Greatest, Bloodiest, Most Decisive Samurai Battle Ever* (2021)

Andrew Gordon, *A Modern History of Japan: From Tokugawa Times to the Present* (2012)

Christopher Harding, *Japan Story: In Search of a Nation. 1850 to the Present* (2000)

Marius B Jansen, *Sakamoto Ryōma and the Meiji Restoration* (1995)

Akamine Mamoru, *The Ryukyu Kingdom* (2018)

Donald S Murray, *For the Safety of All: A Story of Scotland's Lighthouses* (2021)

David Pilling, *Bending Adversity: Japan and the Art of Survival* (2014)

Donald Richie, *The Inland Sea* (1971)

George Sansom, *A History of Japan* (1963)

Acknowledgements

All at Tippermuir – Paul S Philippou, Matthew Mackie (Cover), Rob Hands (Illustrations), Steve Zajda (Proof-reading), Jean Hands (Proof-reading), Bernard Chandler (Graphics).

Ben, Francis, Stephen, Jason, Haruna, Hikaru, and everyone else who accompanied me on these various jaunts. The G-Folk Twitter community who followed and supported me on the trips, often giving helpful local advice. Chris Glenn for correcting my factual errors on the history. Graham Thomas for sharing his research and guiding me to Lake's grave. Scot from Brunton's Craft Beer Bar, Yokohama for geeking out about Brunton with me.

Kosaka Miyuki, for additional research assistance.

Everyone I bored for years about this project whether they asked me what I was working on or not.

And of course, Minori, who humored this daftness.

Lyrics from *Nagasaki* (1929) by Harry Warren and Mort Dixon.

OTHER TITLES
BY TIPPERMUIR BOOKS

Spanish Thermopylae (2009)

Battleground Perthshire (2009)

Perth: Street by Street (2012)

Born in Perthshire (2012)

In Spain with Orwell (2013)

Trust (2014)

Perth: As Others Saw Us (2014)

Love All (2015)

A Chocolate Soldier (2016)

The Early Photographers of Perthshire (2016)

Taking Detective Novels Seriously: The Collected Crime Reviews of Dorothy L Sayers (2017)

Walking with Ghosts (2017)

No Fair City: Dark Tales from Perth's Past (2017)

The Tale o the Wee Mowdie that wantit tae ken wha keeched on his heid (2017)

Hunters: Wee Stories from the Crescent: A Reminiscence of Perth's Hunter Crescent (2017)

A Little Book of Carol's (2018)

Flipstones (2018)

Perth: Scott's Fair City: The Fair Maid of Perth & Sir Walter Scott – A Celebration & Guided Tour (2018)

God, Hitler, and Lord Peter Wimsey: Selected Essays, Speeches and Articles by Dorothy L Sayers (2019)

Perth & Kinross: A Pocket Miscellany: A Companion for Visitors and Residents (2019)

The Piper of Tobruk: Pipe Major Robert Roy, MBE, DCM (2019)

The 'Gig Docter o Athole': Dr William Irvine & The Irvine Memorial Hospital (2019)

Afore the Highlands: The Jacobites in Perth, 1715–16 (2019)

'Where Sky and Summit Meet': Flight Over Perthshire – A History: Tales of Pilots, Airfields, Aeronautical Feats, & War (2019)

Diverted Traffic (2020)

Authentic Democracy: An Ethical Justification of Anarchism (2020)

'If Rivers Could Sing': A Scottish River Wildlife Journey. A Year in the Life of the River Devon as it flows through the Counties of Perthshire, Kinross-shire & Clackmannanshire (2020)

A Squatter o Bairnrhymes (2020)

In a Sma Room Songbook: From the Poems by William Soutar (2020)

The Nicht Afore Christmas: the much-loved yuletide tale in Scots (2020)

Ice Cold Blood (2021)

The Perth Riverside Nursery & Beyond: A Spirit of Enterprise and Improvement (2021)

Fatal Duty: The Scottish Police Force to 1952: Cop Killers, Killer Cops & More (2021)

The Shanter Legacy: The Search for the Grey Mare's Tail (2021)

'Dying to Live': The Story of Grant McIntyre, Covid's Sickest Patient (2021)

The Black Watch and the Great War (2021)

Beyond the Swelkie: A Collection of Poems & Writings to Mark the Centenary of George Mackay Brown (2021)

Sweet F.A. (2022)

A War of Two Halves (2022)

A Scottish Wildlife Odyssey (2022)

In the Shadow of Piper Alpha (2022)

Mind the Links: Golf Memories (2022)

Perthshire 101: A Poetic Gazetteer of the Big County 2022)

The Banes o the Turas: An Owersettin in Scots o the Poems bi Pino Mereu scrievit in Tribute tae Hamish Henderson (2022)

FORTHCOMING

The Whole Damn Town (Hannah Ballantyne, 2022)

Fat Girl Best Friend (Sarah Grant, 2022)

Balkan Rhapsody (Maria Kassimova-Moisset, translated by Iliyana Nedkova Byrne, 2022)

William Soutar: Collected Poetry, Volume I (Published Work) (Kirsteen McCue, Philippa Osmond-Williams and Paul S Philippou (editors), 2023)

William Soutar: Collected Poetry, Volume II (Unpublished Work) (Kirsteen McCue, Philippa Osmond-Williams and Paul S Philippou (editors), 2023)

A British Wildlife Journey (Keith Broomfield, 2023)

The Black Watch from the Crimean War to the Second Boer War (Derek Patrick and Fraser Brown, 2023)

Guid Morning (Lawrence Schimel and Elīna Braslina, Scots translation by Matthew Mackie, 2023)

Madainn Mhath! (Lawrence Schimel and Elīna Braslina, Gaelic translation by Marcas mac Tuairneir, 2023)

Guid Nicht (Lawrence Schimel and Elīna Braslina, Scots translation by Matthew Mackie, 2023)

Oidhche Mhath! (Lawrence Schimel and Elīna Braslina, Gaelic translation by Marcas mac Tuairneir, 2023)

A History of Irish Nationalism and Republicanism in Dundee (c1840 to the Early 1980s) (Ruth Nic Foirbeis, 2023)

Mouse (Avril Duncan, 2024)